REVISE EDEXCEL GCSE (9–1)

History

HENRY VIII AND HIS MINISTERS, 1509–40

REVISION
GUIDE AND WORKBOOK

Series Consultant: Harry Smith

Author: Brian Dowse

A note from the publisher

In order to ensure that this resource offers high-quality support for the associated Pearson qualification, it has been through a review process by the awarding body. This process confirms that this resource fully covers the teaching and learning content of the specification or part of a specification at which it is aimed. It also confirms that it demonstrates an appropriate balance between the development of subject skills, knowledge and understanding, in addition to preparation for assessment.

Endorsement does not cover any guidance on assessment activities or processes (e.g. practice questions or advice on how to answer assessment questions), included in the resource nor does it prescribe any particular approach to the teaching or delivery of a related course.

While the publishers have made every attempt to ensure that advice on the qualification and its assessment is accurate, the official specification and associated assessment guidance materials are the only authoritative source of information and should always be referred to for definitive guidance.

Pearson examiners have not contributed to any sections in this resource relevant to examination papers for which they have responsibility.

Examiners will not use endorsed resources as a source of material for any assessment set by Pearson.

Endorsement of a resource does not mean that the resource is required to achieve this Pearson qualification, nor does it mean that it is the only suitable material available to support the qualification, and any resource lists produced by the awarding body shall include this and other appropriate resources.

For the full range of Pearson revision titles across KS2, KS3, GCSE, Functional Skills, AS/A Level and BTEC visit:
www.pearsonschools.co.uk/revise

Contents

. . . .

A small bit of small print

Edexcel publishes Sample Assessment Material and the Specification on its website. This is the official content and this book should be used in conjunction with it. The questions in *Now try this* have been written to help you practise every topic in the book. Remember: the real exam questions may not look like this.

Society and government

English society in 1509 was very rigid, based on inequality and a social hierarchy where everyone knew their place. This was the England Henry VIII inherited when he became king in 1509.

The social hierarchy of the countryside

In 1509, 94% of the population lived in the countryside.

- Nobility
- Gentry
- Yeomen
- Tenant farmers

Landless or labouring poor

Vagrants, homeless

...and of towns

- Merchants
- Professionals (for example, lawyers, clergy, doctors)
- Business owners
- Skilled craftsmen

Unskilled workers and the unemployed

In 1509, 6% of the population lived in towns.

Many people believed that God had given them their place in society and that they had to **respect** those above them and care for those below them. This meant there were few opportunities for people to improve their position, e.g. becoming a lawyer if they were a skilled craftsman. Most people accepted this and made no attempts to better themselves.

The significance of the wool and cloth trades in England, 1509

Wool trade	Cloth trade
👍 This was a source of wealth for gentry and nobility who owned large flocks of sheep.	👍 Most cloth was woven in Yorkshire, the south-west and the south-east of England. The industry brought wealth to these areas, particularly areas that could also benefit from closeness to the London markets.
👍 Wool was exported, in particular to the Netherlands. This increased the wealth of merchants in port cities like London and Bristol.	👍 The cloth trade was run by merchants who organised themselves into guilds. This enabled them to control the quality of fabrics produced and keep prices high.
👍 Exports increased the wealth of the king and the crown as they levied a tax on each sack of wool exported.	👍 The cloth was exported to Europe, especially the Netherlands and Belgium, and England became the major European cloth producer. By 1540, up to 83% of cloth in Europe came from England.
👎 Landowners enclosed land to graze their flocks, reducing the common land available to ordinary people.	

Structure of government in 1509

The king

Privy Chamber – the king's closest friends

The Royal Household – nobles and servants who advised the king

The Royal Council – nobles and churchmen who helped govern

The Court – nobles who entertained and advised the king

Parliament – passed laws proposed by the king

Justices of the Peace – nobility who kept law and order in different areas of the country

The importance of London

- London was England's biggest city with a population of 60 000. Other large towns included Norwich, Exeter, York and Coventry.

- London was a growing centre of trade, especially weaving and the wool trade. It was also where the king and the royal court were frequently based. Merchants from London traded with Europe including the Netherlands, Spain and Russia.

Now try this

Explain **two** features of English society in 1509.

Henry's accession

Henry VIII gained the throne in 1509, aged 18, and inherited a stable and wealthy kingdom. He had strong views about how he wanted to rule the country, was fit and athletic and had a keen intellect.

The kingdom inherited by Henry

There were no rival contenders to the throne when Henry's father died. This made the throne **secure**. Henry was the second son but his elder brother, Arthur, had died in 1502 and Henry became heir to the throne.

Henry VIII

Henry VII had taxed the nobility heavily and the government coffers were full, but this meant he was unpopular with noblemen who now welcomed a new and less experienced monarch.

The country was a Catholic country, which acknowledged the authority of the pope. It was the pope, and not the king, who controlled the Church and the **Church was extremely powerful**.

Henry the Renaissance Prince

Henry styled himself as a **Renaissance man**, picking up on the revival of culture based on the ideas of ancient Greece and Rome that were sweeping through Europe. Henry had many talents and skills, and also had a keen intellect.

He was a strong athlete. He hunted and practised archery, wrestling and jousting.

He was a musician. He sang, played many instruments and composed.

He spoke French, Spanish and Latin.

He was a good dancer.

Henry VIII, painted by Joos van Cleve.

Henry's views on sovereignty and monarchy

Henry believed:

- he had been appointed by God – this was known as the **divine right of kings**
- people had a duty to obey him
- the monarchy and the court were at the centre of life in England
- in what he thought and said, and it was difficult to convince him otherwise – he was very **stubborn**.

Henry's personal style of government

- Henry used the Royal Council and the Privy Chamber to help him make decisions.
- Henry increasingly made use of one personal adviser or chief minister. Up until 1529 this was Cardinal Wolsey, from 1529 to 1540 it was Thomas Cromwell.
- Henry **delegated** (gave) power as routine tasks bored him – increasing the power of his key advisers, such as Wolsey and Cromwell.

For more on Cardinal Wolsey, see pages 4–11.
For more on Cromwell, see pages 12–19.

Now try this

Give **two** characteristics of Henry's style of government between 1509 and 1529.

 Look at Henry's views on sovereignty as well as his style of personal government.

Henry's strengths, weaknesses and aims

Henry had many strengths but also many weaknesses. When Henry inherited the throne in 1509, he had a number of aims.

Henry's strengths

- **Popular:** he was young and different from his father, who was disliked by noblemen and merchants for imposing high taxes.
- **Popular:** he was handsome and looked like a king.
- **Strong:** he had a team of experienced advisers around him who helped him to rule the country.
- **Strong:** England was stable – there was an established system of government and little threat of rebellion or civil war.
- **Strong:** his wife, Catherine of Aragon, gave Henry strong connections to Spain – a growing European power.
- **Rich:** England was rich and the Crown was not in debt.

A woodcut showing King Henry VIII and his court, possibly by the artist Hans Holbein the Younger.

Henry's weaknesses

- **Naïve:** aged only 18, he had little experience of government.
- **Naïve:** his vision of kingship, based on heroic legends, was simplistic and required him to spend large amounts of money on expensive wars and on his court.
- **Disinterested:** he had little interest in day-to-day government and was happy to delegate power to others. This allowed his ministers to accumulate large amounts of power.
- **Risk taker:** he took part in dangerous sports, such as jousting, which were risky when there was no male successor to the throne.
- **Egotistical and overconfident:** he would not heed advice, leading to costly mistakes.

Henry jousting, with Catherine of Aragon watching on.

Henry's aims

- To create a government where the king decided policy and his ministers carried it out.
- To achieve victory in battles abroad and to become a major force in European affairs.
- To win back lands from France.
- To create a dazzling royal court through dress, architecture and entertainment, comparable with the courts in France and Spain.
- To enhance his prestige by attracting great men to his court, including scholars and artists.
- To be an effective monarch, governing well, maintaining law and order, being committed to the Church and producing a (male) heir who would reduce the risk of civil war on his death.

Now try this

Give **two** advantages that Henry had when he became king.

 Look at Henry's strengths on becoming king.

3

Wolsey's rise to power

Thomas Wolsey was Henry VIII's Lord Chancellor during the first half of his reign.

Timeline

Thomas Wolsey

1473 Born in Ipswich – father was a butcher and a cattle dealer.

1498 He gained a degree at Oxford University and became a priest.

1509 Became a member of the Royal Council as Royal Almoner (in charge of giving money to the poor).

1514 Became Bishop of Lincoln and Archbishop of York.

1515 Became Lord Chancellor and Henry's chief minister, and a cardinal.

1518 Became Papal Legate (pope's representative), becoming the most powerful and senior churchman in the country.

Wolsey started work on rebuilding Hampton Court in 1515. It was taken over by Henry VIII in 1529.

Wolsey's personality

He was:

- not a member of the nobility
- extremely intelligent
- very ambitious
- charming and persuasive, which enabled him to build working relationships with the king and rulers of other countries
- willing to carry out the king's wishes
- ruthless with anyone who threatened him or the king's government
- known as **Alter Rex** (second king) because of his great power and influence.

Wolsey's wealth

Wolsey's power, both in Church and state, and his many jobs allowed him to accumulate enormous wealth. He was 10 times richer than his nearest rival, allowing him to build opulent homes at York Place and Hampton Court where he entertained lavishly.

Wolsey's roles

Wolsey was both Lord Chancellor and a cardinal by 1515. This strengthened his power, as he was able to exert influence over the king and the Church.

The reasons for Wolsey's rise to power

Henry did not involve himself in day-to-day government. This increased Wolsey's power as he was left to carry out the boring but important tasks that Henry wished to avoid.

Wolsey's appointment as Royal Almoner in 1509 made him a member of the Royal Council giving him access to the king. This gave him opportunities to exert influence over Henry and to dominate government by 1515.

Henry disliked many of his father's advisers who he saw as too cautious and unpopular. This removed potential rivals and eased Wolsey's path to power.

Cardinal Wolsey

The war with France in 1512 enabled Wolsey to prove his worth to Henry by organising a well-equipped and well-supplied army by 1513. Wolsey demonstrated skills that Henry later relied on, increasing his power and influence.

Wolsey's persuasive personality and his ability to flatter enabled him to exert influence over the king, while making him an **effective negotiator** on Henry's behalf. His ruthlessness and willingness to financially ruin his rivals deterred any challenges to his position.

Now try this

Explain why Wolsey had become Henry's chief minister by 1515. Give at least **two** reasons in your answer.

Wolsey's reforms

Wolsey carried out a series of important reforms, including laws against enclosure and the reform of the finance and justice systems. He also compiled the **Eltham Ordinances**, which suggested reforms to the Royal Household. Not all of Wolsey's reforms were popular.

Wolsey and enclosure

- Enclosure involved using fences to divide land into fields that were often used to graze sheep, allowing landowners to make money through the wool trade.

- This reduced the land available to tenant farmers (farmers who rented land) and the poor who had less common land to graze their animals.

- Wolsey set up an inquiry in 1517 to investigate this practice and reduce its effect on ordinary people. His work resulted in 260 court cases being brought against landowners.

Wolsey's policies achieved very little as enclosures continued to take place. The policy also angered many landowners, creating enemies for him at court.

Wolsey and the justice system

As Lord Chancellor, Wolsey sought to create a fairer system of justice that ensured the rich (the merchants, gentry and nobility) were not above the law. To achieve this he:

- 👍 strengthened the **Star Chamber** – a royal court that dispensed justice for the king
- 👍 encouraged the poor to bring cases to court
- 👍 increased the court's work rate
- 👍 supported the cases of the poor against the rich
- 👍 oversaw cases himself.

Like the enclosure policies, this reform angered many landowners who accused Wolsey of victimising them.

The Eltham Ordinances, 1526

To tackle the misspending and bad management of the palaces, Wolsey compiled a list of rules 79 chapters long. These included:

- cutting spending on meals and servants
- laying off sick or unneeded servants
- reducing the amount of money paid to people for expenses such as food, fuel and lodgings
- reducing the number of gentlemen in the Privy Chamber from 12 to six.

The Eltham Ordinances were largely unsuccessful, mainly because Wolsey lost interest in them once he had reduced the size of the Privy Council – his main aim.

Wolsey and finance

Wolsey needed to raise money for Henry's battles abroad. There were a combination of old and new methods of taxation used that raised significant amounts of money.

Fifteenths and tenths – these were taxes on moveable goods; 1/15th of their value in rural areas and 1/10th of their value in urban areas.

Crown lands – Wolsey recovered Crown lands from the nobility increasing the income to the government. This raised £15 000 in 1515 alone.

Wolsey's financial measures

The subsidy – this was a tax on incomes (what people earned). This was a progressive tax; the more you earned the more you paid.

Forced loans – Wolsey forced major landowners to lend the government money in 1522 and then again in 1523.

Clerical taxation – this was a voluntary gift made by the Church to the king.

Now try this

Describe **two** ways in which Wolsey improved royal finances up to 1529.

Look at how Wolsey helped the king raise money.

The Amicable Grant

The Amicable Grant was a tax levied on the king's subjects in 1525 to pay for an invasion of France.

Why was the Amicable Grant introduced?

- The King of France had been defeated by Charles V, Holy Roman Emperor, in 1525.
- Henry wanted to take advantage of this by invading France and recovering lands lost by the Crown in the 15th century.
- The Amicable Grant was to help pay for this invasion. It was a tax of a third on the property of priests and of a sixth on the property of ordinary people.

Why was the Amicable Grant controversial?

- Other taxes, including the subsidy, the fifteenth and the tenth had all been approved by parliament. The Amicable Grant had not been approved in this way and was being collected by Royal Decree.
- People only had 10 weeks to pay the tax. Many people resented this demand and could not afford to pay it. There was a risk that people would refuse to pay and the possibility of a rebellion against the king.

For more on the different taxes, see page 5.

The short- and long-term consequences of the Amicable Grant

Short-term consequences

- Many people refused to pay the tax, claiming that they had no money.
- In Lavenham, Suffolk, a full-scale rebellion broke out with 10 000 men gathering in the town expressing their loyalty to the king but demanding he be aware of their anger at having to pay the tax. On the arrival of the Duke of Norfolk and Duke of Suffolk, the rebels surrendered but were pardoned by the king.
- The tax was abandoned.
- Henry postponed the French campaign and made peace with France.

Long-term consequences

- Wolsey was humiliated and his reputation badly damaged. He, rather than the king, had to take responsibility for the tax and its failure.
- Wolsey was unable to raise any further taxes while he remained the king's first minister.
- Henry began, perhaps for the first time, to doubt Wolsey's judgement, beginning a process that would result in Wolsey's fall from power.
- The position of Wolsey's enemies in the royal court was strengthened. Wolsey's introduction of the Eltham Ordinances was perhaps an attempt to reduce their influence over the king.
- The failure of the Amicable Grant demonstrated that there were limitations on the king's power, as he could no longer raise taxes without the consent of parliament.

Wolsey's Amicable Grant failed, damaging his reputation

For more on the Eltham Ordinances, see page 5.

Now try this

Explain **one** short-term and **one** long-term consequence of the Amicable Grant in 1525.

Wolsey's foreign policy aims

Wolsey had a number of policy aims in a Europe dominated by France and Spain. His main aim was to carry out the king's wishes and act as a **peacemaker** between European states.

Europe in the time of Henry VIII

Scotland – an independent country traditionally allied to France in the 'Auld Alliance'. For England, war with France could have meant war with Scotland.

England – a medium-sized power on the edge of Europe. It controlled Wales, Ireland and Calais. English kings traditionally claimed the French throne.

The Holy Roman Empire – a collection of 400 semi-independent states controlled by Charles V, the Holy Roman Emperor, who was also ruler of Spain.

The Ottoman Empire – a powerful Muslim state that was expanding into Europe and North Africa.

Spain – an increasingly powerful and devoutly Catholic country ruled by Charles I who was also the Holy Roman Emperor (Charles V). Spain and the Holy Roman Empire became known as the **Habsburg Empire**.

France – the most populous kingdom in Europe. It was ruled by Francis I who had a fierce rivalry with the Habsburgs.

England's position in Europe was helped by the rivalry between Charles V and Francis I. Charles V was a potential ally in any war with France, while Francis I would be an ally in any conflict with Charles V. If Charles and Francis made peace, then England would be diplomatically isolated and vulnerable.

Wolsey's aims abroad

- To create better relationships with both France and the Habsburg Empire. This would prevent England being **diplomatically isolated and vulnerable**.
- To play Europe's two major powers (the Habsburg Empire and France) off against each other to England's advantage.
- To provide opportunities for Henry to gain military glory, enhancing his prestige, while making sure that wars did not become too expensive.
- To allow Henry to be seen to be a major peacemaker. This would enhance his prestige without the expense of long wars.

Henry was desperate for military glory, but wars were expensive and required taxes that undermined the king's popularity. They were also risky as the king's reputation could be at stake if armies were defeated and land lost.

For more on taxes, see pages 5 and 6.

Now try this

Why was Wolsey cautious about involving England in a long war in Europe?

Think about the cost of any conflict in which England might become involved.

Foreign policy outcomes

Initially, Wolsey's foreign policy was successful. However, after 1522, it began to run into difficulties as both Charles V and Francis I proved to be unreliable allies.

Timeline

1512 England and Spain form an anti-French Alliance.

1518 Treaty of London.

1521 Treaty of Bruges.

1525 French army defeated at the Battle of Pavia and Francis I taken prisoner.

1528 England and France declare war on Charles V.

1512–14 Henry's first war with France – Battle of the Spurs.

1520 Henry and Francis I meet at the 'Field of the Cloth of Gold'.

1522–25 Henry's second war with France.

1525–29 Anglo-French Alliance.

1529 Treaty of Cambrai.

Up to 1525, England was an ally of the Holy Roman Empire against France. Following the Battle of Pavia, Henry allied with France against the Holy Roman Empire.

Wolsey's successes 1514–22

At the start of his time as Henry's chief adviser, Wolsey had successes:

1 **1514** The Battle of the Spurs was the final battle in the first French war that ultimately gave victory to Henry.

2 **1518** The **Treaty of London** was a diplomatic triumph for Wolsey as he initiated it. It promised universal peace by proposing that each state followed a non-aggressive foreign policy by not attacking each other. If one power did go to war, they would be at risk of other countries coming to the aid of the country being attacked. The treaty:
- was signed by 20 European leaders and the pope
- brought prestige to Henry
- placed Henry and Wolsey at the centre of European politics.

This only prevented war for three years.

3 **1520** The 'Field of the Cloth of Gold' was one of a series of diplomatic meetings arranged by Wolsey. Francis I and Henry met near Calais. It was a splendid showcase for the two kings and an impressive display of English power and wealth, putting Henry at the centre of European diplomacy. Nothing was decided or agreed at the meeting.

Wolsey's failures, 1522–29

During the 1520s, Wolsey experienced increasing difficulties in foreign affairs with France and the Holy Roman Empire.

1 **1522–25** French war and alliance with Charles V failed because Wolsey's support for Charles V against France, in the **Treaty of Bruges**, was based on the idea that Charles would help him seize French territory and the French throne. This did not happen. Charles gave Henry little military support. After the Battle of Pavia, Charles ignored Henry's suggestion that France be divided between England and the Holy Roman Empire with Henry getting the French throne. Instead, Charles released Francis from captivity. The war was unpopular, cost £430 000 and achieved little.

2 **1525–29** An alliance with France to fight Charles V failed because the French were again defeated by Charles and received little help from England, damaging Henry's reputation as a reliable ally.

In 1529, Francis I negotiated a peace deal with Charles V in the **Treaty of Cambrai**, only notifying Wolsey of the negotiations when it was too late. This was a snub to Wolsey and Henry and left them diplomatically isolated.

The unreliability of Francis I and Charles V was a key factor in Wolsey's disastrous foreign policy.

Now try this

Explain, in fewer than 150 words, how Wolsey's diplomacy ran into difficulties after 1522.

Catherine of Aragon and the succession

Henry's marriage to Catherine of Aragon in 1509 initially worked well. However, Catherine's failure to provide him with a son meant that Henry become uncertain of his marriage.

Henry's marriage to Catherine

The marriage was successful because:

✓ Henry was a loving and affectionate husband

✓ Catherine was a popular queen due to her charitable work

✓ Catherine was supportive of Henry; she acted as regent when Henry was fighting the French between 1512 and 1514. She even dispatched an army to Scotland to defeat and kill James IV, sending Henry James' bloody shirt as a gift.

✓ it strengthened Henry's relationship with Spain and the Holy Roman Empire. This improved England's prospects in any war against France as it would have the support of Spain and would not be isolated in Europe.

For more on the French war, 1512–14, see page 8.

Catherine's failure to provide Henry with a son

Catherine was pregnant at least six times between 1509 and 1520, but only one child, Princess Mary, survived. Catherine's failure to provide Henry with a male heir was a growing concern to him because:

- it reflected badly on Henry's manhood and reputation, and suggested that Henry was incapable of producing a male heir

- it threatened the succession as the absence of a male heir encouraged others from both inside and outside the kingdom to consider claiming the throne – this raised the prospect of invasion and civil war

- Catherine was six years older than Henry and by 1527 was 42 years old, making another pregnancy and a male heir unlikely.

All Catherine's fault?

Catherine's failure to provide Henry with a male heir led him to question his marriage.

Catherine of Aragon, painted c1530.

1. Henry blamed Catherine for not giving him a healthy son – he had had an illegitimate son by his mistress, Bessie Blount, so it couldn't have been his fault.

2. Henry had lost interest in Catherine and had turned his attentions to younger women, including Anne Boleyn.

3. By marrying his dead brother's wife (Catherine had briefly been married to Prince Arthur), Henry thought God was punishing him by not giving him a male heir, as in the Old Testament it states: 'If a man shall take his brother's wife it is an impurity... they shall be childless.'

How to end the marriage

The only way that Henry could end his marriage was through an **annulment** leading to a divorce. This was a problem.

- Only the pope could approve an annulment.

- An annulment/divorce would upset Charles V who was Catherine's nephew.

- Catherine would resist an annulment because it would imply that she was no more than the king's mistress, while her daughter, Mary, would lose her claim to the throne.

An annulment is a legal term suggesting the marriage was never valid and had never existed.

Think about the consequences of the failure to provide Henry with a son.

Now try this

Why was the issue of the succession important to Henry VIII?

Attempts to gain an annulment

Henry sought to annul his marriage to Catherine of Aragon but was opposed by Pope Clement VII, Catherine and her nephew, Charles V.

In 1527, Henry instructed Wolsey to persuade Pope Clement VII to grant an annulment on the grounds that the marriage was ungodly (against scripture) and that the original papal dispensation allowing the marriage to happen was incorrectly worded.

Pope Clement VII was reluctant to grant the annulment as he did not want to offend Charles V whose troops were close to Rome.

In 1528, Wolsey proposed that, as Papal Legate, he would rule on the case along with the pope's representative, Cardinal Campeggio. This failed because, under the pope's instructions, Campeggio dragged out proceedings. In July 1529, the case was **adjourned** without a decision being reached.

Throughout this time, tremendous pressure was placed on Catherine to **renounce** her marriage to Henry. It was suggested that she give up the crown and become a nun, and she was accused of hating the king. Henry also threatened to ignore their daughter, Princess Mary, excluding her from the succession.

A case is **adjourned** when it is stopped without a decision being reached.

The court case and opposition to the annulment

The court case was held at Blackfriars court, London, between June and July 1529.

Catherine was popular with ordinary people due to her charitable work.

Catherine had the support of Thomas More, adviser to the king.

Catherine had the support of John Fisher, Bishop of Rochester.

Henry recognised Catherine's support and had to tread carefully in his dealings with her, making it difficult to annul the marriage without papal approval.

Catherine was resolutely opposed to the annulment and even publicly begged the king not to cast her aside. This made it hard for Henry to make a convincing case for annulment.

Cardinal Campeggio engaged in delaying tactics, frustrating Henry and Wolsey by refusing to come to a decision on the issue and, in the end, saying it was for Rome to decide after all.

Now try this

Give **two** reasons why Wolsey failed to annul Henry's marriage to Catherine of Aragon by 1529.

Wolsey's fall from power

Wolsey fell out of favour with Henry for a number of reasons, the main ones being the failure of the divorce proceedings in London, in 1529, and the growing influence of the Boleyn family at court.

Amicable Grant
Wolsey's decision to introduce the Amicable Grant tax in 1525 damaged his reputation as it led to a rebellion and the failure to collect the tax. Henry was forced to distance himself from Wolsey's actions, undermining his power and influence over the king.

Wolsey's reforms
Wolsey's reforms to the justice system, his opposition to enclosure, his willingness to reclaim land held by the nobility for the Crown and his high-handed nature had made him many enemies at court. These people were more than happy to conspire with the Boleyns to undermine Wolsey.

Wolsey's fall from power in 1529

Annulment
Wolsey's failure to secure an annulment of Henry's marriage to Catherine angered Henry. He became increasingly impatient with Wolsey and began to believe that he was working with the pope to prevent an annulment from happening.

The Boleyns
Henry's infatuation with Anne Boleyn gave the Boleyn family, especially her father Thomas Boleyn and her brother, George, increasing influence at court. Wolsey's failure to secure an annulment led them to plot against him by suggesting to Henry that Wolsey was siding with the pope and not interested in securing an annulment. Anne hated Wolsey and, together with her brother and other nobles who were unhappy with Wolsey, persuaded Henry to get rid of him.

Foreign policy
Wolsey's failure to build an alliance against Charles V was frustrated by the Treaty of Cambrai, leaving England isolated and vulnerable in Europe. Henry was prepared to get rid of Wolsey because he no longer had confidence in his skills as a diplomat.

For more on the Amicable Grant, see page 6. For more on Wolsey's foreign policy, see pages 7 and 8. For more on Wolsey's reforms, see page 5. For more on the annulment, see pages 9 and 10.

Wolsey's dismissal

- In October 1529, Wolsey was stripped of most of his powers and possessions and exiled to York.

- In July 1530, Wolsey was summoned to London on charges of **praemunire** (working in the interests of the pope and not the king), but died on his way down to London to face trial.

Court politics

- Wolsey had remained in power for so long because he was able to ensure that other courtiers had little influence over the king.

- However, Henry's infatuation with Anne Boleyn ended this. It allowed a rival camp, the Boleyns, to emerge in court.

- The Boleyns were able to work with Wolsey's other enemies to **undermine** his authority and influence over the king.

Now try this

Read through the reasons why Wolsey fell from power. Put the reasons in order, starting with what you think was the main reason.

Cromwell's early career

Thomas Cromwell, who was not a member of the nobility, rose from very humble beginnings to become the king's chief minister by 1534.

Timeline

Cromwell's background and early career

1485 Born in Putney. His father was an innkeeper.

1503–14 Travelled and worked in Europe, mainly Italy, and then as a cloth merchant in Antwerp.

1514–19 Returned to England and married Elizabeth Wyckes. Became a successful merchant and lawyer in London.

1519 Became a member of Wolsey's council and became a trusted adviser.

1529 Became MP for Taunton.

1531 Became a member of the **Privy Council**.

Having travelled and lived in Europe, Cromwell became increasingly influenced by Protestant (Reformist) ideas, which shaped his thinking on the annulment, the Church and the monasteries.

Cromwell's personality

👎 Cromwell is often seen as a ruthless and unprincipled figure who was prepared to do the king's 'dirty work', such as organising the execution of members of the nobility and dissolving the monasteries.

👍 In reality, Cromwell was capable of great loyalty to his friends and, indeed, to his predecessor, Wolsey.

👍 Cromwell had a vibrant personality and could be witty, charming and persuasive when he wanted or needed to be.

Thomas Cromwell, painted by Hans Holbein the Younger. Cromwell is often seen as a dark figure in history, although in reality he had a warmer side to his personality.

The reasons for Cromwell's rise to power

Loyalty
Cromwell remained loyal to Wolsey, defending him in parliament and even in audiences with the king. This loyalty impressed Henry who was prepared to promote Cromwell on the grounds that he would be equally loyal to Henry, as a servant of the king.

Wit and charm
Cromwell's wit and charm won him many supporters at court, including the king.

Ruthlessness
Cromwell's ruthlessness meant that the king was prepared to rely on him to manage violent and controversial acts and discouraged rivals and opponents from challenging his power.

Efficiency
As Henry began to involve himself more in day-to-day government after 1530, Cromwell was there to carry out his instructions quickly and efficiently and as the king's loyal servant.

Now try this

Was Cromwell's ruthlessness the real reason why he secured Henry's confidence? Write a paragraph to explain your ideas.

 Think about Cromwell's strengths and not just his ruthlessness.

Cromwell and the king's annulment

Cromwell became the king's chief minister in 1534. His handling of the annulment of Henry's marriage to Catherine of Aragon played a key part in Cromwell's success.

How Cromwell managed the annulment of Henry's marriage to Catherine

Anne Boleyn in 1534

1. Cromwell quickly realised that Pope Clement VII was not willing to annul Henry's marriage to Catherine as he did not want to upset Charles V.

2. Cromwell, therefore, changed tactic, arguing that the power to grant an annulment should be taken from the pope and given to Henry instead.

3. Henry and Anne Boleyn were secretly married by Archbishop Cramner in January 1533. This was important because Anne was already pregnant and there was a need for the child to be a **legitimate heir** to the throne.

4. Parliament passed the Act in Restraint of Appeals in March 1533, asserting that England was an empire and not subject to any form of foreign rule. Henry was now head of the Church and only he, and not the pope, could annul his marriage to Catherine.

5. A divorce hearing began in May 1533 in a court led by Archbishop Cranmer. The court announced that:
   - the pope's legal dispensation allowing Henry to marry Catherine was invalid
   - Henry and Catherine had never been legally married
   - Henry's secret marriage to Anne was valid because he had been a bachelor at the time.

6. Anne was crowned as Henry's queen in a royal coronation and gave birth to a daughter, Elizabeth, in September 1533.

 By arranging these events, Cromwell had shown that he had huge influence over Henry.

Cromwell's roles and responsibilities after 1534

After the success of the annulment, Henry entrusted Cromwell with further powers. As Henry's chief minister, Cromwell's influence over the king increased.

In charge of the Church
Became Vicar-General in 1535, with power to institute Church reform.

In charge of king's personal seal
Became Lord Privy Seal in 1536, a senior position in the Privy Council with unlimited access to Henry's documents.

Cromwell 1534–40

Influential role in law
Had become Master of the Rolls in 1533.

In charge of finances
Had become Chancellor of the Exchequer in 1533.

In charge of Henry's household
Became Lord Great Chamberlain in 1540.

Now try this

Describe how the success of the annulment was beneficial to Cromwell's career.

 Think about the relationship between Cromwell and Henry.

The fall of Anne Boleyn

Anne Boleyn was executed in May 1536, only three years after her coronation as queen. Cromwell played a major role in her downfall.

Timeline

The events leading up to Anne's execution

September 1533 Anne gave birth to a daughter, Elizabeth. This disappointed Henry as it was not the son and heir he wanted.

1534 Anne had a miscarriage.

January 1536 Anne had another miscarriage and the foetus was thought to be deformed, convincing many in the court that Anne was a witch.

2 May 1536 Following an investigation by Cromwell, Anne was charged with adultery and treason and taken to the Tower of London. She was accused of having affairs with Mark Smeaton (a court musician), courtiers Sir Francis Weston, Sir Henry Norris and Sir William Brereton and her brother, George Boleyn.

15 May 1536 Anne was found guilty.

17 May 1536 Anne's marriage to Henry was annulled.

19 May 1536 Anne was executed.

Only Mark Smeaton admitted to an affair with Anne. His confession is unreliable as he was almost certainly tortured, possibly in Cromwell's presence.

The Beheading of Qg:Anne Bullen.

The execution of Anne Boleyn at the Tower of London in 1536. Anne was in fact executed by a sword and not by an axe as this image suggests.

Reasons for Anne's fall

1. By early 1536, Henry was becoming infatuated with Jane Seymour and saw her as his queen and not just his mistress. Anne would have to be removed to make way for Jane.

2. Henry was becoming increasingly exasperated with Anne. She had failed to provide him with a male heir, while her assertive personality and flirtatious behaviour in court may have become an embarrassment to him, making him want to be rid of her.

3. Anne had strong opinions about foreign policy and religion that were not considered seemly and this increasingly irritated Henry.

4. There was a poisonous atmosphere in court with gossip circulating. Anne had many enemies who may have been prepared to peddle allegations of adultery, which Henry was more than happy to believe.

Cromwell's role in Anne's fall

Some historians believe that Cromwell deliberately conspired to bring down Anne:

- Cromwell was aware of Anne's role in the downfall of Wolsey and did not want to share his fate.
- Anne and Cromwell had differences of opinion on foreign policy and how the income gained from the **dissolution of the monasteries** should be spent.
- Cromwell built the case for adultery against Anne, interviewing and torturing witnesses and using spies in the queen's own bedchamber to unearth any evidence of adultery. Cromwell was able to use this evidence to persuade Henry and the court that Anne was guilty.

However, others believe it was unlikely that Cromwell conspired to end Anne's time as queen as they had much in common. It would seem that by Cromwell building a case against Anne he was simply carrying out Henry's wishes to be rid of her.

Now try this

Giving **two** reasons, explain why Anne Boleyn was executed in 1536.

Jane Seymour

Jane Seymour married Henry and became queen on 30 May 1536, 11 days after Anne Boleyn's death. She gave birth to a male heir, but died shortly afterwards.

The marriage

Henry was keen to marry Jane as quickly as possible because he needed a child (and preferably a son) to become the **legitimate heir** to the throne. Without this, there was a risk that if Henry died, the succession would go to someone outside of the family.

There was no longer an heir to the throne because:

- Princess Mary and Princess Elizabeth had been declared illegitimate – both their mothers' marriages to Henry had become invalid

- Henry Fitzroy, Henry's illegitimate son, had died soon after the **Act of Succession** had been passed in 1534, this was unfortunate because the Act allowed Henry to appoint any successor he liked and he could have appointed Henry Fitzroy.

For more about the Act of Succession of 1534, go to page 21.

Jane Seymour, 1536, painted by Hans Holbein the Younger. Henry was genuinely attracted to her – she was kind and obedient and was disinterested in politics (unlike Anne).

The heir

✓ Jane fulfilled her royal duty on 12 October 1537 by giving birth to a son, Edward (later to become Edward VI).

✓ This strengthened the succession and there was less chance of **competing claims** for the throne on Henry's death.

✓ The birth also strengthened Henry's authority because it suggested God had blessed Henry with a son, implying that his marriage to Jane and the events that preceded it (the execution of Anne and the annulment of his marriage to Catherine) were acceptable to God.

See pages 9 and 10 for more about Henry's marriage to Catherine of Aragon and its annulment. For more about the execution of Anne Boleyn, turn to page 14.

The death

Less than two weeks after giving birth to Edward, Jane died. Henry went into a state of mourning and refused to marry again for another two years.

In spite of this, the search to find a new wife for Henry started once more. He needed to marry again to produce more male heirs. A new marriage would also form the basis of an alliance with other European powers, helping to challenge the combined threat posed by Francis I and Charles V.

Jane's marriage to Henry gave the Seymour family a higher status within the royal court. Jane's brothers made the most of this, in particular Edward, who was appointed to the Privy Council. After Jane's death, the brothers, as uncles to Henry's heir, continued to be influential in court. Edward became an adviser to Henry, as well as first Earl of Hertford and later Duke of Somerset.

Now try this

Give **two** reasons why the birth of Edward VI was important.

 Consider the importance of the succession to Henry.

Cromwell's reforms

Cromwell made a number of changes to government and finance, including reform of the Royal Council; reform of the Council of the North; improvements to the government of Wales; and financial reforms.

Reform of the Royal Council

Cromwell argued that the Royal Council was too big as it contained up to 100 members.

- Cromwell replaced it with a new, simpler body known as the Privy Council, made up of about 20 permanent advisers.
- The Privy Council was increasingly composed of lawyers and professional administrators, rather than noblemen.
- Cromwell hoped that this would stop one person dominating, as all would have equal status and working experience.
- A clerk to the Privy Council was appointed to record decisions.

Reform of the Council of the North

- The Council of the North had existed since 1472 and aimed to improve how the North of England was governed. It contained members of the nobility and churchmen. It had met from time to time under previous kings.
- Cromwell made it into a permanent institution, which from 1537 was responsible for maintaining law and order in the North.
- The Council was an important means by which rebellion was prevented and the government's authority maintained. This was especially important after the Pilgrimage of Grace, which challenged Henry's authority.

For more on the Pilgrimage of Grace, see pages 28 and 29.

Financial reforms

Traditionally, the **King's Chamber** was used to record the income (taxes, rents, etc.) and expenditure (money spent) of the king and his government. With the increase in income from the dissolution of the monasteries, Cromwell decided the Chamber couldn't cope with the increased work, so he created six departments. Four dealt with the king's traditional income, and two dealt with the increased work created by the dissolution:

1 **The Court of Augmentations**, which dealt with property and income from the dissolution of the monasteries.

2 **The Court of First Fruits and Tenths**, which collected taxes from the clergy previously sent to the pope in Rome.

Each department had the power to settle financial disputes and was given its own budget. They were run by well-trained officials who were monitored by others to ensure that they were doing their jobs properly.

For more on the dissolution of the monasteries, see page 26.

Reform of Wales, 1536

Wales became officially part of England and English law replaced Welsh law.

English was declared the official language in Wales.

Map legend:
- The Principality
- New counties

Counties shown: ANGLESEY, CAERNARFON, MEIRIONNYDD, DENBIGHSHIRE, FLINTSHIRE, CHESHIRE, SHROPSHIRE, MONTGOMERYSHIRE, CARDIGAN, RADNORSHIRE, ENGLAND, HEREFORDSHIRE, PEMBROKESHIRE, CARMARTHEN, BRECON, GLAMORGAN, MONMOUTHSHIRE, GLOUCESTERSHIRE

0   50
Kilometres

Wales was represented by 26 MPs.

The Welsh March was divided up into new counties, each of which was controlled by a Justice of the Peace (JP).

The purpose of these reforms was an attempt to tackle disorder in Wales, as well as secure the support of the Welsh gentry by giving them the same powers as their English equivalents.

The importance of the reforms

- ✓ He created a professional civil service, no longer run by nobles and clergy.
- ✓ Power was centralised in London.
- ✓ The role of the Exchequer was increased and expenditure monitored by government officials and not by the king.
- ✓ Government was better organised.

Now try this

Describe **two** ways in which Cromwell changed how England was governed between 1534 and 1540.

The management and use of parliament

Cromwell developed the role and importance of parliament as a means of making the laws of the land, which would strengthen the government's authority.

Henry's personal style of government

Henry's style of government was to make his own decisions about things through the Royal Council. The decisions were pronounced by **royal proclamation** and he expected people to obey him. Cromwell wanted to change this.

Parliament at the start of Henry VIII's reign

☑ Parliament had existed since the 13th century.

☑ It contained two chambers: the House of Lords (made up of landowners and bishops) and the House of Commons (made up of gentry and merchants).

☑ Its role was limited to approving taxation.

☑ It did not meet very often.

For more on Henry's early style of government, see page 2.

The development of the role of parliament by Cromwell

- Cromwell used parliament more regularly.
- Key changes in the Church and the state were made by Acts of Parliament (statute law).
- The king and Cromwell used parliament to gain support from the people who were significant: the nobility and churchmen in the House of Lords; and the merchants and gentry in the House of Commons. This strengthened the king's authority as it suggested that these people approved of his ideas and policies by turning them into laws.

Cromwell's effectiveness in managing parliament

For this system to work, Henry and Cromwell had to ensure that there was support in parliament for the laws they wanted to pass. Cromwell achieved this by:

- controlling parliamentary business, ensuring that ideas were debated and discussed and laws properly **drafted** (put together and worded properly)
- sitting as an MP, which enabled him to guide debates and ensure that there was support for the laws he wanted to pass
- using threats and intimidation to undermine any opposition.

The significance of the increased use of parliament

Henry's early personal style of government	Style of government after Cromwell's reforms of parliament
Parliament had a limited role in making decisions.	Parliament was at the centre of government – it had legislative power and could pass laws on all aspects of daily life.
Laws were passed by the king and the Royal Council.	Laws were passed with approval of both houses of parliament and the king – this strengthened the king's authority.
Parliament was not consulted on all matters.	Parliament could not be ignored and had to be consulted on all major laws the king wanted to pass.

Now try this

Give **two** consequences of Cromwell's growing use of parliament. The table above will help you.

Anne of Cleves

Cromwell's reputation was badly damaged by the failure of Henry VIII's marriage to Anne of Cleves.

Reasons for, and the significance of, the marriage

1. By 1539, there seemed to be a real threat of a combined Catholic crusade against England launched by Charles V (ruler of Spain and the Holy Roman Empire) and Francis I (ruler of France). A marriage to Anne of Cleves would provide Henry with a valuable European ally, who might persuade other German states to help him if England was attacked.

2. Unlike many European rulers, the Duke of Cleves seemed happy to marry Anne off to Henry, as he and other reformist states needed allies against Charles V. This was in spite of Henry's marred reputation as someone who had killed his wife.

3. Henry had still only one male heir – Edward. The risk of Edward dying young required a further marriage to produce more male heirs.

4. The Duke of Cleves had also broken from Rome, so this suggested that Henry had no intention of backing out of his decision to break from Rome too.

Anne of Cleves

Anne was the second daughter of the Duke of Cleves, a small state in the north of the Holy Roman Empire. She was 24 years old when she came to England and spoke very little English.

A miniature of Anne of Cleves, painted by Hans Holbein the Younger and sent to Henry. Henry found this representation of her attractive and wanted to 'nourish love' by marriage. However, when he met her in person he took an immediate dislike to her, referring to her as a 'Flanders mare'.

Cromwell's role in the marriage

Cromwell was a reformer sympathetic to Protestant ideas. He believed that, by marrying Henry to Anne, the Protestant cause would be strengthened in court. Therefore, he encouraged Henry to accept this match.

Henry gave permission for marriage negotiations to begin and a marriage treaty was signed in October 1539.

⬇

However, when Anne arrived in England in December 1539, Henry took an instant dislike to her. He shouted at Cromwell, 'I like her not! I like her not!'

⬇

Despite being postponed, the marriage went ahead on 6 January 1540 after persuasion from Cromwell.

The failure of the union had the effect of weakening the Protestant cause in court, resulting in Henry demanding a return to Catholic values.

The failure of the marriage and the downfall of Cromwell

By the summer of 1540, the threat of invasion from France and the Holy Roman Empire had declined and Henry no longer needed an alliance with the Duke of Cleves. He had also become attracted to Catherine Howard, one of the queen's ladies-in-waiting.

The marriage was annulled on the grounds of non-consummation after just four months. Anne was granted estates by the king and became known as the king's 'sister'.

Henry blamed Cromwell for the failure of the marriage. This made Cromwell vulnerable to rivals at court, such as the Duke of Norfolk (Catherine Howard's uncle), who wished to remove Cromwell from power.

Now try this

Why did the marriage between Henry and Anne of Cleves reduce Cromwell's influence in court?

Think about who Henry would have blamed for the failure of the marriage and why.

Cromwell's fall

Thomas Cromwell was executed on 28 July 1540 for treason. Henry had blamed him for the failure of his marriage to Anne of Cleves but had awarded him the title of Earl of Essex in April 1540, so Cromwell would seem to have still been in favour. It was the role of the Duke of Norfolk who largely led to his downfall.

The fall of Cromwell

On 15 June 1540, Cromwell was arrested at a Privy Council meeting, accused of treason and heresy. The Duke of Norfolk allegedly ripped the seals of office from around Cromwell's neck, while all his goods, valued at £7000, were confiscated by the state.

⬇

Cromwell was taken to the Tower of London and parliament passed an Act of Attainder on 29 June, condemning him to death without trial.

⬇

In spite of a letter proclaiming his innocence and pleading for 'mercy, mercy, mercy!', Cromwell was executed on 28 July on the same day that Henry married Catherine Howard.

The Duke of Norfolk

Thomas Howard, the 3rd Duke of Norfolk, was the uncle of Catherine Howard who became Henry's fifth wife in 1540. He was a fierce rival of Thomas Cromwell and had ambitions of his own to become the king's chief minister. Being a Catholic, the Duke of Norfolk was hostile to the Protestant cause.

The Duke of Norfolk was a key player in Cromwell's fall from power.

The influence of the Duke of Norfolk

The Duke of Norfolk hated Cromwell because:

- Cromwell supported Protestant ideas
- he was jealous of Cromwell's rise from a humble background, in particular when he became an earl
- Cromwell had such an influence over Henry.

Seeing the failure of Anne's marriage, Norfolk recognised his chance to stir things up and sour the relationship between Cromwell and Henry.

The Duke of Norfolk:

- instructed his niece, Catherine Howard, to spread rumours about Cromwell, saying he was being inefficient in arranging the annulment of Henry's marriage to Anne of Cleves
- claimed that the delay was because Cromwell wanted to introduce Protestantism to England against the king's wishes.

Other reasons for Cromwell's fall

1 Cromwell was hated by French Catholics, especially Francis I, who saw him as a **heretic** and supporter of Charles V. Removing Cromwell from power would lead to improved relations with France and reduce the possibility of any Catholic crusade against England.

2 Cromwell had many enemies within the court and in the Church. They resented his dissolution of the monasteries, the execution of John Fisher and Thomas More, as well as his support for the cause of reform and moving England to become Protestant. They were more than happy to vote in parliament for the **Act of Attainder** that led to Cromwell's execution. To them, Cromwell was an 'evil counsellor' who had misled the king.

For more on John Fisher and Thomas More, see pages 22 and 23.

He was under pressure from the Duke of Norfolk.

He was under pressure from the Church.

Henry's decision to execute Cromwell

He was under pressure from the court.

Ill-health made Henry bad tempered and led him to make hasty decisions.

⬅ In 1541, Henry claimed he had been deceived by his courtiers and regretted the death of his 'most faithful servant'.

Now try this

Give **three** reasons for Cromwell's fall from power in 1540.

Henry and the Catholic Church

In the early stages of his reign, Henry remained loyal to the Catholic Church and hostile to Protestantism. However, by 1534, Henry had renounced the pope's authority and split with Rome.

The Reformation in Europe

During the Reformation (led by a German priest called **Martin Luther**) the Christian Church in Europe split between Catholics and Protestants as described in the following table:

Catholics	Protestants
Catholics accepted the authority of the pope as head of the Church.	Protestants rejected the pope's authority and believed that rulers, including monarchs, should instead lead and protect their own churches.
The Church's main job was to deliver the seven sacraments (Church ceremonies) as a display of devotion to God.	They argued that the Church's principal function was to preach the word of God in the Bible. Only three sacraments mattered: the Eucharist; baptism; and penance.
Catholics believed in **transubstantiation**, arguing that the bread and wine actually becomes the body and blood of Jesus.	The bread and wine only represented the body and blood of Jesus – they did not become his body and blood.
Church services and readings from the Bible were said in Latin.	Church services and Bible readings were in the language of the country so that ordinary people could understand them.
Chantries (prayers for the dead) and indulgences (certificates forgiving sins) could be purchased to shorten the time spent in purgatory before entering heaven.	Chantries and indulgences were seen as corrupt and unnecessary – faith alone was required to get you into heaven.
Images and statues were venerated (regarded as sacred and prayed to) in Catholic churches.	Praying to images and statues was seen as superstitious; they were unwelcome in churches.
Pilgrimages were a good way of gaining God's approval.	Pilgrimages were unnecessary.
Priests wore special clothing (vestments) to set them apart from ordinary people.	Priests were ordinary people and could wear ordinary clothes.
Priests were not allowed to marry.	Priests were permitted to marry.

Henry as 'Defender of the Faith'

At first, Henry was supportive of the Catholic cause and hostile to Protestantism.

- He wrote a book called In *Defence of the Seven Sacraments*, which led to Pope Leo X describing him as '**Defender of the Faith**' in 1521.
- Luther's texts were publically burned by Wolsey in a pyre built at St Paul's churchyard in London.

Reasons for Henry's campaign against the Catholic Church

Henry wanted to increase his power over the Church because of:

1 the pope's failure to annul his marriage to Catherine of Aragon

2 the impact of Protestant ideas – many of his advisers were sympathetic to the new ideas and he particularly liked the idea of William Tyndale, who suggested that the Church should be ruled by kings

3 allegations of corruption in the Church.

Now try this

What other reasons were there, other than the pope's failure to annul his marriage to Catherine of Aragon, for Henry's campaign against the Catholic Church?

The Acts of Succession and Supremacy

Henry was able to introduce an English Reformation by taking control of the English Church through the Act of Succession, 1534, and the Act of Supremacy, 1534.

Henry's laws to control the Church

Law	Its significance
The Act of Succession, 1534 This stated that only children from Henry's second marriage to Anne Boleyn could inherit the throne. This meant that his daughter, Mary, became illegitimate and his second daughter, Elizabeth, became the true heir to the throne.	This was a final rejection of the pope's right to decide whether someone could divorce or remarry. It also amounted to a rejection of the pope's authority in England, as the pope's name was crossed out of all English prayer books.
The Act of Supremacy, 1534 This established that the king and not the pope controlled the English Church; Henry became the Supreme Head of the English Church – he now had the powers previously held by the pope.	Henry could decide: • how the Church was organised • the Church's religious beliefs • who was appointed to important positions within the Church, including bishops. It also meant that Henry now controlled the Church's income and wealth. He was now in a position to sell Church property and seize Church taxes leading to the setting up of the Court of Augmentations and the Court of First Fruits and Tenths. For more on Church taxes, see page 5.

Cromwell's role in enforcing the Acts

Cromwell was appointed Vicar-General, enabling him to wield the powers that belonged to the king to deal with anyone who spoke out against Henry, the split with Rome or Henry's control of the Church. It was hoped that people would be so frightened of **retribution** (punishment) there would be no dissent.

Beauchamp Tower prison in the Tower of London where many high profile prisoners accused of treason were kept.

Oath of Succession (a clause in the Act of Succession) All individuals, including churchmen, were required to take an Oath of Succession recognising Anne Boleyn's right to be queen. Failure to do so was seen as an act of treason and could be punishable by death.

The Treason Act 1534 Treason was traditionally defined as plotting the king's death, waging war against him or helping his enemies. The Treason Act 1534 expanded this definition to include speaking out against the royal supremacy. People who did so could now suffer a traitor's death (hanging, drawing and quartering).

Now try this

Explain why the Acts of Succession and Supremacy were important for Henry's control of the English Church.

Use Henry's laws to control the Church to help you.

Elizabeth Barton and John Fisher

Henry's changes to the Church were challenged by Elizabeth Barton, the Nun of Kent, and John Fisher, Bishop of Rochester. They were both subsequently executed.

Elizabeth Barton, the Nun of Kent

- Elizabeth Barton was a nun who, when seriously ill, claimed to have had a vision of the Virgin Mary who cured her.
- Many people, including members of the nobility and the gentry, regarded her as a holy woman possessed of miraculous powers who ought to be taken seriously.

John Fisher

- John Fisher became Bishop of Rochester in 1504.
- He was a famous scholar who tutored Henry when he was a young prince.
- In 1535, the pope made Fisher a Cardinal.

The death of Elizabeth Barton

What Elizabeth Barton did	How Henry reacted	What happened next
• From 1527, Barton's visions became sinister, criticising Henry for his proposed divorce from Catherine of Aragon. Barton said that God had told her the king would die a villain's death. • She criticised Protestant ideas saying that people should remain loyal to the pope and burn English translations of the Bible. • In 1533, Dr Edward Bocking published the *Nun's Book*, which contained a collection of Barton's prophecies claiming that Henry would burn in hell.	• This posed a serious threat to Henry because it could inspire people, in a superstitious age, to resist Henry's reforms, creating the possibility of rebellion. Therefore, Henry ordered Cromwell to act. • Barton's visions were also an embarrassment to Henry.	• In July 1533, Barton and her accomplices were interrogated. • On 23 November 1533, Barton was forced to confess to lying about her visions. • She was condemned by attainder – an Act of Parliament that allowed people to be executed without trial. On 21 April 1534, Barton was executed for treason. • This took place on the same day as Londoners took the Oath of Succession. This was a warning of what would happen if they didn't. • All 700 copies of the *Nun's Book* were burned.

The death of John Fisher

1 Fisher condemned Henry's attempts to secure a divorce as well as his split from Rome. → Even though Henry hated Fisher he hadn't broken any laws, so there was nothing Henry could do. → Henry remained suspicious of Fisher and watched him closely.

2 Fisher had links with Elizabeth Barton. → Henry could have arrested Fisher for treason because of his links with Barton. → However, Fisher was fined £300 instead.

3 Fisher refused to take the Oath of Succession in April 1534. → Henry sent Fisher to the tower. → Fisher was executed for treason in June 1535, a few months after he had been made a cardinal by the pope.

Now try this

Give **two** reasons why Henry treated Barton and Fisher so harshly.

Opposition from Thomas More

Sir Thomas More, who became Henry VIII's Lord Chancellor after the fall of Wolsey, was executed in July 1535 for treason for refusing to take the Oath of Succession.

Sir Thomas More

Sir Thomas More (centre) and his family, painted by Hans Holbein the Younger.

Thomas More:

- was a scholar and a great Renaissance thinker renowned throughout Europe. His greatest work was a book called *Utopia* describing a perfect society.

- was a devout Catholic who saw Protestants and Martin Luther as criminals who 'bespatter the most holy image of Christ crucified with the most foul excrement of their bodies'.

- actively suppressed Protestantism by burning Protestant books and, as Chancellor between 1529 and 1532, hunted down and interrogated suspected Protestants whom he accused of heresy. Six Protestants were burned to death during his time of office.

Timeline

More's arrest and execution

13 April 1534 Henry feels that because More does not openly support him he is against him, so forces him to take the Oath of Succession. More refuses to do so.

1 July 1535 After over a year in prison and after several visits from Cromwell trying to persuade More to take the oath, More is placed on trial where evidence is heard that he had indeed spoken his true feelings about Henry and the break from Rome. This evidence, though probably made up, was enough to find him guilty of treason.

1532 More resigns from being Chancellor because he can no longer support Henry in his determination to divorce Catherine of Aragon and renounce the authority of the pope. More retires from public life.

17 April 1534 More is sent to the Tower of London where he refuses to explain why he will not take the oath. By not explaining why, his tactic is that he will not be committing treason.

6 July 1535 More is executed on Tower Hill.

The significance of Thomas More's opposition

More was one of Europe's great intellectuals and his death outraged many in Europe, including Charles V, and discredited Henry, making a Catholic crusade against England more likely.

More became a martyr for the Catholic cause, encouraging unrest and rebellion.

The execution of Thomas More was designed as a signal to the nobility that no one was beyond the reach of the king.

The trial and execution created an atmosphere of terror in England as people feared the consequences of speaking out against the king.

The execution deepened the split with Rome as the pope threatened to excommunicate Henry.

Now try this

Give **two** reasons why More's opposition to Henry's religious reforms was important.

The impact of the Reformation on the Church

Between 1534 and 1540 there was conflict in the English Church between those who wanted to make the Church more Protestant and those who wished to retain Catholic beliefs and practices. Cromwell and Archbishop Cranmer wished to point the Church in the Protestant direction, while Henry continued to practise his Catholic beliefs, despite his break with Rome.

The English Church in 1534

- The Act of Supremacy made Henry head of the English Church at the expense of the pope.
- This gave Henry the power to change the Church's beliefs and practices.
- Both Reformers (Protestants) and Catholics tried to influence the way in which Henry chose to shape the Church.
- The Reformers hoped to remove Catholic beliefs and practices such as transubstantiation and pilgrimages. Catholics tried to keep them.

Reformers v Catholics

Reformers	Traditional Catholics
Thomas Cromwell	Thomas Howard, Duke of Norfolk
Archbishop Thomas Cranmer	Stephen Gardiner, Bishop of Winchester

They had to be cautious not to declare themselves Protestant.

They had to be cautious, as denying royal supremacy would be seen as treason.

Cromwell, Cranmer and moving the Church towards Protestantism

Cromwell and Cranmer worked together to change the Church slowly and gradually.

1. **Act of Ten Articles, 1536**
2. **Royal Injunctions, 1536**
3. **Bishops Book, 1537**
4. **Royal Injunctions, 1538**

1. This set out the beliefs of Henry's new church. It reduced seven sacraments to three: the Eucharist or Communion; baptism; and penance.

2. This tried to ensure that all priests practised the same thing: to speak in favour of the royal supremacy and discourage pilgrimages. The number of Holy Days was also reduced.

3. This was another attempt to set out the beliefs of the Church. Many Catholic beliefs were given less importance. It stated the main duty of a priest was preaching.

4. This declared that every church should have a Bible translated into English and that all holy relics, statues and images were to be destroyed as well as pilgrimage sites.

Henry's continuation of Catholic beliefs

Henry felt that reform had gone far enough and, in 1539, published the Six Articles reaffirming traditional Catholic beliefs such as transubstantiation, clerical celibacy (priests abstaining from marriage and sex) and purgatory. Failure to agree to these would lead to imprisonment, confiscation of property and death. Many Protestant ideas had found their way into the Church, but with the death of Cromwell the Protestant cause was weakened.

For more on Cromwell's death, see page 19.

One paragraph might focus on how the country had become more Protestant and the second on how it still remained Catholic.

Now try this

'In 1540, England had become a Protestant country.' How far do you agree with this judgement? Write two or three paragraphs explaining your ideas.

The role of religious houses

At the start of Henry's reign in 1509, England had 800 religious houses served by over 10 000 monks and nuns. These played a prominent role in local communities.

Types of religious houses (monasteries)

✓ Large religious houses were known as abbeys under the control of an abbot (monk) or abbess (nun). These included Westminster, Tewkesbury and Glastonbury.

✓ Medium-sized houses were called priories (monks) or nunneries (nuns).

✓ The smaller houses were known as friaries (monks).

Most religious houses were historic institutions that had existed since the Middle Ages. They were run by different orders which had their own rules that monks and nuns had to obey.

Monasteries in the community

Reconstruction of how Thetford Priory would have looked in 1540.

Many monasteries were very wealthy institutions. They owned about one-third of all land in England and the top 20 monasteries had incomes of £1000 per year, comparable with many members of the nobility. Monasteries were often an important part of local communities and were sometimes endowed (paid for) by local landowners.

Religious – monasteries acted as places of religious contemplation. Monastic rules required monks to engage in worship and prayer on a daily basis. To ensure that they worshipped God properly, monks were expected to be poor, chaste and obedient. Monks and nuns also said prayers for the dead known as chantries.

Places of refuge – monasteries were safe places where people could stay when they travelled. They also acted as safe havens for people who felt threatened.

Commercial – many large monasteries were businesses controlling estates and renting out land to local farmers.

Educational – monks often educated young boys of the nobility and gentry. Monasteries also acted as places of learning and where manuscripts and books were written and kept.

Monasteries carried out a range of different roles and functions

Administrative – some senior monks helped administer local justice and 30 sat in the House of Lords. Some advised the king.

Medical – monasteries also acted as hospitals and hospices looking after the sick and the dying.

Social and economic – monasteries provided help for the poor. They also provided employment for local people who helped run the monasteries and maintain their lands. In addition, monasteries provided a home for widows and widowers, as well as elderly nobles.

Now try this

Describe the role played by monasteries towards the poor in early 16th-century England.

Remember that monasteries carried out a range of different roles.

The dissolution of the monasteries

The **dissolution** (closing down) of the monasteries took place for a range of different reasons. These were religious, financial and political.

Reasons for the dissolution of the monasteries

Religious – many reformers, including Cromwell and Cranmer, disapproved of many of the religious practices in the monasteries, including prayers for the dead. Getting rid of the monasteries would, in their view, end these backward practices.

Political – Henry VIII may have felt that many monks and nuns were loyal to the pope rather than the king. This seemed to be confirmed by the fact that many religious houses had supported the Pilgrimage of Grace. Closing down the monasteries would strengthen Henry's control of the Church by getting rid of sources of opposition within it.

For more on the Pilgrimage of Grace, see pages 28–30.

Fountains Abbey in Yorkshire was closed down in 1539.

Financial – the monasteries were very wealthy. Closing down the monasteries, taking over and renting out the land would benefit Henry financially as:

- it would pay for any future wars and the defence of England against any Catholic crusade organised by Francis I and Charles V
- it would make him financially independent of parliament and Henry would no longer have to ask it to approve taxation
- land could be sold off or given as gifts to the nobility to win over landowners previously hostile to Henry's control of the Church.

Many historians argue that because Henry kept many Catholic beliefs his motivation for getting rid of the monasteries was financial and political rather than religious.

How the monasteries were dissolved

In 1535, Cromwell commissioned a survey into the workings of the smaller monasteries and nunneries.

⬇

This led to a series of visitations (inspections) of monasteries. These alleged that monks were not keeping to their strict moral code as they kept mistresses, engaged in homosexual practices, gambled and, in the case of nuns, bore children. The survey also confirmed the wealth of the monasteries giving a combined total of £160000 per year.

 It was later proved that many of the more bizarre claims made by the inspectors were exaggerated or untrue.

⬇

The **Act for the Dissolution of the Lesser Monasteries** in 1536 closed the smaller monasteries and nunneries.

⬇

A further series of visitations in 1538 led to many abbots and abbesses surrendering their religious houses as a gift to the king. This was confirmed by the **Act for the Dissolution of the Greater Monasteries** in 1539.

Now try this

'Henry's real reasons for getting rid of the monasteries were financial.' How far do you agree with this statement? Write no more than 200 words.

 Remember to examine all of Henry's motives.

Beneficiaries and losers

Beneficiaries (winners) of the dissolution of the monasteries were the king, the nobility and the reformers. However, for many devout Catholics, the poor and tenant farmers the impact of the closure of monasteries was significant.

The beneficiaries

1 Religious reformers like Cromwell and Cranmer
- The closure of the monasteries meant that a powerful symbol of the Catholic Church was brought to an end.
- Dissolution was another step along the road towards a reformed Church.

2 Henry VIII
- The wealth accrued by the dissolution of the monasteries made Henry financially independent and very rich.
- The closure of the monasteries helped end opposition from within the Church to his rule.

3 The nobility
- They received monastic lands from the king either as a gift or sold to them cheaply.
- They could now farm the land commercially, increasing their incomes and wealth.

Examples of the types of treasures sold off or destroyed with the dissolution of the monasteries.

The losers

1 Monks lost their homes and livelihood. While many monks were re-employed by the Church, many suffered unemployment and hardship.

2 Nuns lost their homes and livelihood. Nuns weren't able to work in churches or marry, so suffered great hardships, resorting in many cases to begging.

3 Devout Catholics mourned the end of Catholic practices such as prayers for the dead (chantries) performed in monasteries.

4 The poor and sick had nowhere to go if they could not provide for themselves or fell ill. Many became beggars and vagrants.

5 Tenant farmers who had rented land from the monasteries saw rents rise or they were thrown off the land by the gentry.

So many monks, nuns and tenant farmers losing their livelihoods and homes in a short space of time led to towns being swamped with beggars and homeless people.

Cultural impact of the dissolution

Loss of:
- 👎 historical buildings
- 👎 beautiful artefacts
- 👎 centres of learning with libraries destroyed.

Establishment of:
- 👍 cathedral grammar schools and university colleges to replace monastery schools.

Some abbeys became cathedrals, such as Westminster Abbey.

Now try this

Who benefited most from the dissolution of the monasteries, and who benefited least? Make a list in order, starting with those who benefited most.

Pilgrimage of Grace: reasons

The Pilgrimage of Grace was a major uprising (rebellion) that started in the North of England in 1536.

The Pilgrimage of Grace

- A series of rebellions took place in Yorkshire (under Robert Aske) and Lincolnshire (under Nicholas Melton).

- Minor rebellions also took place in Cumberland and Westmoreland.

- The participants viewed themselves not as rebels but as Christ's soldiers aiming to restore Catholicism or the 'old religion' to England.

- They wanted to negotiate with the king and did not want to fight him.

For more on the events of the rebellion, see page 29.

The badge showing the five wounds of Christ worn by those on the Pilgrimage of Grace.

Religious
Fear that the attack on the 'old religion' would continue and parish churches would be next.

Social
Anger at the closure of the monasteries that led to, among other things, hunger and homelessness and no help for the sick.

Political
Resentment at Cromwell's interference in local affairs and his attempts to centralise power.

Reasons for the Pilgrimage of Grace

Economic
Resentment:

- at continuing taxation with the 1534 Subsidy Act still being collected
- at rising rents
- at increase in enclosure
- by landowners towards the Statute of Uses introduced in 1536 – a tax on inheritance.

Also, bad weather had led to a poor harvest, increasing dissatisfaction.

Key characters

Leaders of the rebellion
Robert Aske – a lawyer
Nicholas Melton – a shoemaker
Lord Darcy – a nobleman

Henry's men
Charles Brandon, Duke of Suffolk
Thomas Howard, Duke of Norfolk

Pilgrims on the Pilgrimage of Grace march, 1536.

Now try this

Monasteries were an important part of life in the early 16th century. How did the Pilgrimage of Grace demonstrate this?

 Look at who supported the Pilgrimage of Grace and why it happened.

Pilgrimage of Grace: key events

The Pilgrimage of Grace began with the Lincolnshire rebellion and was followed by the Yorkshire rebellion, the Pontefract Articles and the defeat of the uprising.

Key dates, events and routes of the Pilgrimage of Grace

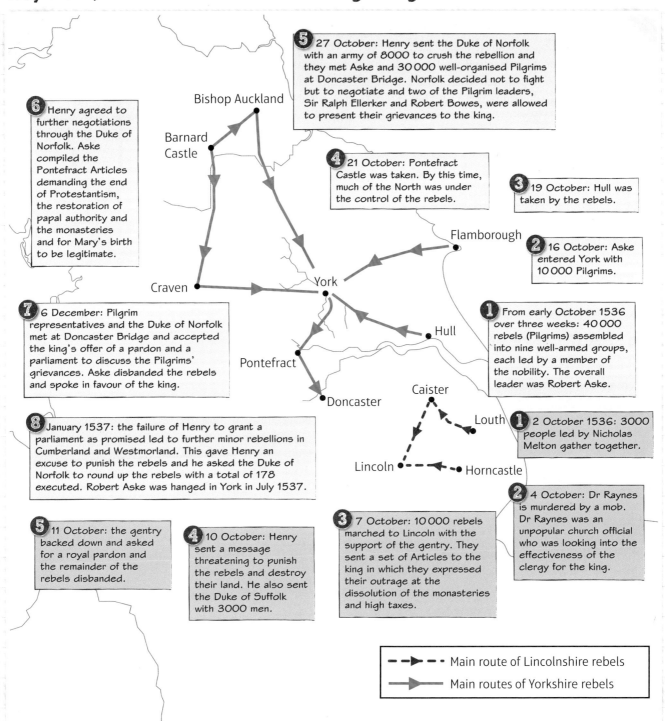

5 27 October: Henry sent the Duke of Norfolk with an army of 8000 to crush the rebellion and they met Aske and 30 000 well-organised Pilgrims at Doncaster Bridge. Norfolk decided not to fight but to negotiate and two of the Pilgrim leaders, Sir Ralph Ellerker and Robert Bowes, were allowed to present their grievances to the king.

6 Henry agreed to further negotiations through the Duke of Norfolk. Aske compiled the Pontefract Articles demanding the end of Protestantism, the restoration of papal authority and the monasteries and for Mary's birth to be legitimate.

4 21 October: Pontefract Castle was taken. By this time, much of the North was under the control of the rebels.

3 19 October: Hull was taken by the rebels.

2 16 October: Aske entered York with 10 000 Pilgrims.

1 From early October 1536 over three weeks: 40 000 rebels (Pilgrims) assembled into nine well-armed groups, each led by a member of the nobility. The overall leader was Robert Aske.

7 6 December: Pilgrim representatives and the Duke of Norfolk met at Doncaster Bridge and accepted the king's offer of a pardon and a parliament to discuss the Pilgrims' grievances. Aske disbanded the rebels and spoke in favour of the king.

1 2 October 1536: 3000 people led by Nicholas Melton gather together.

8 January 1537: the failure of Henry to grant a parliament as promised led to further minor rebellions in Cumberland and Westmorland. This gave Henry an excuse to punish the rebels and he asked the Duke of Norfolk to round up the rebels with a total of 178 executed. Robert Aske was hanged in York in July 1537.

2 4 October: Dr Raynes is murdered by a mob. Dr Raynes was an unpopular church official who was looking into the effectiveness of the clergy for the king.

5 11 October: the gentry backed down and asked for a royal pardon and the remainder of the rebels disbanded.

4 10 October: Henry sent a message threatening to punish the rebels and destroy their land. He also sent the Duke of Suffolk with 3000 men.

3 7 October: 10 000 rebels marched to Lincoln with the support of the gentry. They sent a set of Articles to the king in which they expressed their outrage at the dissolution of the monasteries and high taxes.

Map labels: Bishop Auckland, Barnard Castle, Craven, York, Flamborough, Hull, Pontefract, Doncaster, Caister, Louth, Lincoln, Horncastle

- – ▶ - – Main route of Lincolnshire rebels
- ───▶ Main routes of Yorkshire rebels

Now try this

Explain why the Duke of Norfolk had to negotiate with the Pilgrims rather than crush them by force?

Think about how much support the rebels had and how Henry needed time to defuse the rebels.

Failure of the uprising

The Pilgrimage of Grace was unsuccessful because of Robert Aske's misplaced faith in the king. It was highly unlikely Henry would give in to the rebels as this would have weakened his control and power considerably.

The failure of the Pilgrimage of Grace

1 Robert Aske's misplaced faith in the king led to the undoing of the uprising. Aske was prepared to accept Henry's offer of a pardon and a parliament to discuss the rebels' complaints. This meant that the rebel army was disbanded, removing the threat to Henry's throne. It also gave Henry the time he needed to plan a way of crushing the rebels in 1537.

2 Henry's ruthlessness also helped to end the rebellion. Henry could not accept the rebels' demands as this would have made him appear weak, encouraging others to challenge his authority. It would also have completely undermined his religious policy. Henry, therefore, was bound to destroy the rebellion and violently put to death its perpetrators to reinforce his authority, preserve his religious policy and discourage any other potential rebellions.

The heads of executed rebels on stakes were a stark warning to people that Henry would deal ruthlessly with anyone who challenged his authority.

The significance of the Pilgrimage of Grace

It threatened the king
It was the largest uprising of Henry's reign. It involved 40 000 men and the capture of castles and cities in the North of England. At the end of 1536, it represented a very real threat to Henry's position as king, as the rebel army could have moved southwards towards London, driving him from his throne.

It sped up the closure of the monasteries
Henry recognised that many of the monasteries had backed the rebellion and were opposed to his policies. This meant that Henry sped up the dissolution, closing down the larger abbeys as well as the smaller religious houses.

It postponed plans to carry out religious reform
It demonstrated that the North of England remained staunchly Catholic and that many people rejected Henry's religious policies. This made it dangerous for both Henry and Cromwell to introduce reformist (Protestant) policies and reforms were postponed – a knock back to Cromwell's plans.

It strengthened the Council of the North
It demonstrated that Henry needed to strengthen his grip on the North to prevent further rebellions from occurring. This led to a strengthening of the Council of the North.

For more on the Council of the North, see page 16.

Now try this

'The Pilgrimage of Grace failed because Robert Aske put too much faith in the king.' Give a reason why you agree/disagree with this statement.

Exam overview

This page introduces you to the main features and requirements of the Paper 2 Option B3 exam.

About Paper 2

- Paper 2 is for both your period study and your British depth study.
- Henry VIII and his ministers is a British depth study – it will be in Section B of Paper 2: Medieval depth options.
- Henry VIII and his ministers is Option B3. You will see where it starts on the exam paper with a heading like this:

Option B3: Henry VIII and his ministers, 1509–40

The Paper 2 exam lasts for 1 hour 45 minutes (105 minutes) in total. There are 32 marks for the period study and 32 marks for this depth study, so you should spend about 50 minutes on each.

The three questions

The three questions for Option B3 will always follow this pattern.

Question 4(a)

Describe **two** features of … 　　　　　(4 marks)

Question 4(a) targets Assessment Objective 1 (AO1): it focuses on describing features.

Assessment Objective 1 is where you show your knowledge and understanding of the key features and characteristics of Henry VIII and his ministers, 1509–40.

You can see examples of all three questions on the next six pages, and in the practice questions on pages 38–49.

Question 4(b)

Explain why … 　　　　　(12 marks)

Two prompts and your own information

Question 4(b) targets both AO1 and AO2. It focuses on causation: explaining why something happened.

Question 4(c)

Choice of two questions:
(c)(i) or (c)(ii)

[Statement] How far do you agree? Explain your answer. 　　　　　(16 marks)

Two prompts and your own information

You have a choice of two questions for 4(c). These target both AO1 and AO2. You need to make a judgement in this question.

Assessment Objective 2 is where you explain and analyse key events using historical concepts such as causation, consequence, change, continuity, similarity and difference.

Question 4(a): Describing features 1

Question 4(a) on your exam paper will ask you to 'Describe **two** features of...'. There are 4 marks available for this question: two for each feature you describe.

Worked example

Describe **two** features of the Act of Supremacy (1534).

(4 marks)

 You can revise the Act of Supremacy on page 21.

What is a feature?

A **feature** is something that is distinctive or characteristic – we can tell one person from another, for example, because of their distinctive facial features. When a question asks for two features of something, think about the special characteristics of that something.

Sample answer

Feature 1
The Act gave Henry control of the Church's religious beliefs, income and wealth.

Feature 2
The Act made Henry Supreme Head of the English Church because he wanted its wealth and resources.

 The student has written one feature of the Act of Supremacy.

 The student has written an **explanation** of why the Act of Supremacy was imposed. As this is a description question, this explanation is not relevant here.

For this question make sure you identify two **different** features. There are no extra marks for extra features. This answer also needs more supporting information.

Improved answer

Feature 1
One feature of the Act of Supremacy was that it gave Henry complete control of the Church of England. It was Henry VIII, rather than the pope, who controlled the Church's beliefs, liturgy and wealth.

 The student has correctly identified a feature of the Act of Supremacy (that it gave Henry control of the Church) and has added good supporting information.

Feature 2
Another feature of the Act of Supremacy was that it greatly increased the government's income and wealth. The Crown could now, using the Court of Augmentations and the Court of First Fruits and Tenths, seize Church taxes and property. This boosted the king's income and made him less dependent on parliament for money.

 The student has now just picked one feature and added relevant detail to it in a way that demonstrates their knowledge of the topic and their understanding of how the Act of Supremacy worked.

Question 4(a): Describing features 2

Question 4(a) on your exam paper will ask you to 'Describe **two** features of...'. There are 4 marks available for this question: two for each feature you describe.

Worked example

Describe **two** features of Henry's marriage to Anne of Cleves (1540).   **(4 marks)**

 You can revise Henry VIII's marriage to Anne of Cleves on page 18.

What does 'describe' mean?

Describe means to give an account of the main characteristics of something. You develop your description with relevant details, but you do not need to include reasons or justifications.

Sample answer

Feature 1
Henry's marriage to Anne of Cleves was an arranged marriage.

Feature 2
When Henry met Anne of Cleves, he disliked her and decided that he did not want to marry her.

 This is a correct feature of the marriage, but the answer is rather basic and does not demonstrate enough knowledge.

 This does describe events connected to the marriage, but it needs to be refocused so that it describes a feature: a special characteristic of the marriage.

 Specific detail has been included – Henry's dislike of Anne of Cleves – but more support is needed to back up the description.

Improved answer

Feature 1
Henry's marriage to Anne of Cleves was an arranged marriage. Marriage negotiations began after Henry was sent a flattering portrait of Anne. A marriage treaty was then signed in October 1539.

Feature 2
Henry did not want to complete the marriage. When he met Anne, who seemed indifferent to him and not as beautiful as suggested in the portrait he had received, Henry uttered, 'I like her not!' The initial marriage ceremony was then postponed and did not take place until January 1540.

 Detail has been added to describe the key feature, which is the arranged marriage negotiation.

 This has now been refocused to describe how Henry's dislike of Anne nearly prevented the marriage from going ahead.

Question 4(b): Explaining why 1

Question 4(b) on your exam paper is about causation: explaining why. There are 12 marks available for this question and two prompts to help you answer. You must also use information of your own.

Worked example

Explain why Wolsey fell from power in October 1529. **(12 marks)**

You may use the following in your answer:
- the influence of the Boleyns
- the failure to annul the marriage to Catherine of Aragon.

You **must** also use information of your own.

What does 'explain' mean?

Explain means saying how or why something happened, backed up with examples or justifications to support the reasons you give. A good way to get into an explanation is to use sentence starters, such as 'One reason for this was...', or 'This was because...'.

 Links You can revise the reasons for Wolsey's fall from power on page 11.

Compare this answer with an improved version on the next page.

Sample answer

Wolsey fell from power in October 1529 when he was stripped of his offices and wealth before being exiled to York. This was due to a number of reasons: the failure to annul the marriage to Catherine of Aragon; the growing influence of the Boleyns; and the Treaty of Cambrai.

Wolsey had failed to annul Henry's marriage to Catherine of Aragon by 1529 as Pope Clement VII, scared of Charles V, had refused to do so. Henry still remained married to Catherine. He could not divorce her and marry Anne Boleyn.

The Boleyns' influence in court was also growing. Both George and Thomas Boleyn were often seen at court and did not like Wolsey.

The Treaty of Cambrai took place in 1528 between France and the Holy Roman Emperor, Charles V. Europe's two main Catholic powers would no longer go to war with each other.

The first paragraph of the answer is very strong. It relates directly to the question and sets up a clear line of argument.

The second paragraph follows one of the prompts: failure to annul the marriage to Catherine of Aragon. The student demonstrates good factual knowledge (AO1), but does not use this knowledge in an explanation (AO2). This section should be **explaining** why the failure to secure an annulment led to Wolsey's fall from power.

The third paragraph picks up the other prompt of the question: the influence of the Boleyns. Again, the student demonstrates good factual knowledge, but there is only one point at which the student hints at an explanation: 'and did not like Wolsey'. This is not enough: details should be used to support the explanation, not the other way round.

 Own information is brought into the final paragraph: 'took place in 1528 between France and the Holy Roman Emperor'. This is a real strength of the answer. However, the information provided is not linked closely enough to the question.

Question 4(b): Explaining why 2

This page has an improved version of the answer on the previous page.

Improved answer

Wolsey fell from power in October 1529 when he was stripped of his offices and wealth before being exiled to York. This was due to a number of reasons: the failure to annul the marriage to Catherine of Aragon; the growing influence of the Boleyns; and the Treaty of Cambrai.

By 1529, Wolsey had failed in his mission to secure an annulment of Henry's marriage to Catherine of Aragon as the pope, Clement VII, did not want to upset the Holy Roman Emperor, Charles V. This frustrated Henry as he remained wedded to Catherine and could not marry Anne Boleyn, produce a son and secure the succession. This diminished Henry's confidence in Wolsey, as he could not negotiate effectively with the pope or his legate, leading to his fall from power.

This can be linked to the growing influence of the Boleyns at court. Neither George nor Thomas Boleyn liked Wolsey, who they saw as deliberately seeking to disrupt and delay the annulment proceedings. They were, therefore, able to exploit Henry's growing sense of frustration over the annulment, encouraging him to remove Wolsey from office.

This growing distrust of Wolsey was further strengthened by the Treaty of Cambrai in 1528 between Francis I and Charles V. This left England dangerously isolated in Europe, facing two potentially hostile powers: France and the Habsburgs. This would have further discredited Wolsey in the eyes of Henry, leading to his fall from power, as he could no longer be trusted to conduct diplomacy on behalf of the king.

Analysis is about examining something carefully in order to identify the reasons that explain it. The most successful answers to 4(b) questions provide an **analytical explanation**. This means a tight focus on what the question is asking, and careful selection of reasons that provide a well-thought-through explanation.

Causation questions

Question 4(b) is about causation – causes. These questions have 6 marks for AO1 (accurate and relevant information) and 6 marks for AO2 (explanation and analysis). Strong answers combine explanation and analysis (AO2) with relevant information (AO1).

This is an improved version of the answer on the previous page.

This first paragraph is not changed as it provides a strong introduction and sets up the student's analysis of the question.

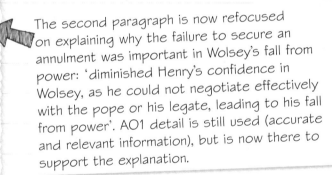
The second paragraph is now refocused on explaining why the failure to secure an annulment was important in Wolsey's fall from power: 'diminished Henry's confidence in Wolsey, as he could not negotiate effectively with the pope or his legate, leading to his fall from power'. AO1 detail is still used (accurate and relevant information), but is now there to support the explanation.

The third paragraph also now has a focus on **explaining how** the influence of the Boleyns contributed to Wolsey's fall from power by being 'able to exploit Henry's growing sense of frustration'.

In the final paragraph, the student uses their own knowledge to give an example of how the Treaty of Cambrai undermined confidence in Wolsey.

Question 4(c): Making a judgement 1

Question 4(c) on your exam paper involves analysing the statement in the question and deciding how far you agree with it. There are 16 marks available for this question and two prompts to help you answer. You must also use information of your own.

Worked example

'The main reason Cromwell fell from power in 1540 was the failure of the marriage between Henry and Anne of Cleves.'

How far do you agree? Explain your answer.

(16 marks)

You may use the following in your answer:
- the role of the Duke of Norfolk
- the marriage to Anne of Cleves.

You **must** also use information of your own.

Links You can revise the fall of Cromwell on page 19.

Analysing the statement

Question 4(c) will always include a statement, which may start with phrases such as 'The main reason for...' or 'The main consequence of...'. You decide whether or not you agree by considering whether other aspects or reasons, or other consequences, were more important.

Remember, for question 4(c) you will choose to answer either option (i) or option (ii).

Sample answer

Compare this answer with an improved version on the next page.

The marriage to Anne of Cleves resulted in divorce and contributed to Cromwell's fall from power. However, other factors are important, including the role of the Duke of Norfolk and the need to improve relations with France.

The first paragraph of this answer is very strong and sets out the key argument clearly.

Cromwell played a key role in persuading Henry to marry Anne of Cleves as a means of gaining European allies. Henry, however, did not find Anne 'The Flanders Mare' attractive and married her only reluctantly. Henry quickly wanted a divorce and blamed Cromwell for what happened.

The second paragraph contains good subject knowledge and suggests that the marriage to Anne of Cleves was important, but does not link the failure of the marriage to Cromwell's fall from power.

The Duke of Norfolk was also important in Cromwell's downfall. He despised Cromwell's lowly birth. He was related to Catharine Howard, who Henry now wished to marry, and may have persuaded Henry that Cromwell was delaying a divorce to Anne as well as trying to make England a Protestant country.

It is becoming clear that the student is not being **analytical** enough. Instead of considering other possible reasons for Cromwell's fall, weighing up their importance and linking them to his fall from power, they are only listing possible reasons why Cromwell's position was weakened by 1540.

Finally, many Catholics, including the French king, Francis I, loathed Cromwell who was seen as a heretic and a key figure in the dissolution of the monasteries.

The ideas set out in the introduction are not being developed and sustained across the answer.

Question 4(c): Making a judgement 2

This page has an improved version of the answer on the previous page.

Improved answer

The marriage to Anne of Cleves resulted in divorce and contributed to Cromwell's fall from power. However, other factors are important, including the role of the Duke of Norfolk and the need to improve relations with France.

The failed marriage to Anne of Cleves undoubtedly encouraged Cromwell's fall from power. Cromwell encouraged Henry to marry Anne as a mean of securing a diplomatic alliance with the Duchy of Cleves that may in turn have led to alliances with other (Protestant) German states. The problem was that Henry's hopes of marrying the physically attractive woman, documented in Holbein's miniature, were dashed by her appearance and behaviour leading to the postponement of the marriage until January 1540 and a rapid divorce afterwards. The whole affair was both expensive and embarrassing to Henry. This only served to undermine Henry's confidence in Cromwell, leading to his fall from power.

Yet other factors contributed to Cromwell's demise. The Duke of Norfolk disliked Cromwell due to his lowly birth as well as the dissolution of Thetford Abbey where his ancestors were buried, giving him a motive to plot against Cromwell. The fact that Henry found the Duke's niece, Catherine Howard, attractive gave Norfolk greater influence over Henry at court, enabling him to persuade Henry that Cromwell was deliberately delaying the divorce proceedings and was plotting to make England a Protestant country. This undermined Cromwell's position in court leading eventually to his loss of office and execution. The fact that Henry claimed in 1541 that he had been misled over the death of 'his most faithful servant' suggests that Norfolk had a major influence in Cromwell's arrest and execution.

Finally, the diplomatic situation in 1540 also undermined Cromwell. Many Catholics in Europe, including Francis I, disliked Cromwell who they saw as a heretic responsible for the deaths of More and Fisher, as well as the dissolution of the monasteries. Removing and executing Cromwell would satisfy Europe's Catholics, reducing the possibility of a Catholic crusade launched by France and/or the Holy Roman Emperor, Charles V.

In conclusion, the failed marriage to Anne of Cleves was important but was not the only reason for Cromwell's fall. The actions of the Duke of Norfolk and the need to satisfy Europe's Catholic rulers were also important factors in his fall.

The balance of Assessment Objectives

Question 4(c) is worth 16 marks in total:
- 6 marks are for AO1
- 10 marks are for AO2.

This shows the importance of analysis and explanation. AO1 information and understanding also needs to be combined with AO2 explanation and analysis for the best results.

The student has again summarised the key points in the first paragraph, setting up the analysis which makes up the rest of the answer.

This is an improved version of the answer on the previous page.

Remember, you need to make a judgement when answering question 4(c).

Now the answer considers other factors that may have been important, and also evaluates how significant the divorce from Anne actually turned out to be.

The solid analysis provided by the student then leads up to a judgement at the end that the student can justify.

Had a go ☐   Nearly there ☐   Nailed it! ☐

Practice

Put your skills and knowledge into practice with the following question.

Option B3: Henry VIII and his ministers 1509–40

Answer Question 4(a), 4(b) and **EITHER** 4(c)(i) **OR** 4(c)(ii).

4 (a) Describe **two** features of the Treaty of London (1518).

(4 marks)

Feature 1

   The Treaty of London (1518) required each of the

20 countries who signed it to pursue a non-aggressive

foreign policy.

....

....

....

Feature 2

....

....

....

....

....

....

You have 1 hour 45 minutes for the **whole** of Paper 2, so you should spend about **50 minutes** on this option. Remember to leave 5 minutes or so to check your work when you've finished writing.

Links You can revise the Treaty of London on page 8.

You need to identify **two** valid features and support each feature with evidence.

An example of a suitable feature might be that: 'The Treaty of London established a system of collective security.' A suitable supporting statement could be: 'If one power went to war, it risked being attacked by the other countries who had signed the treaty.'

Your exam paper will have a separate space for each feature you need to describe.

'Describe' means you have to give an account of the main characteristic. You do not need to explain why the feature was important or what it was trying to achieve.

Practice

Put your skills and knowledge into practice with the following question.

4 (b) Explain why the Pilgrimage of Grace took place in 1536.   **(12 marks)**

You may use the following in your answer:

- the dissolution of the monasteries
- rising rents and taxes.

You **must** also use information of your own.

Remember that question 4(b) is all about causation: this means you are looking for relevant reasons.

....

....

....

....

Links You can revise the Pilgrimage of Grace on pages 28–29.

....

....

....

....

....

For example, you might explain that the dissolution of the monasteries angered many people **because** they provided people with employment and somewhere to go when they became sick. They also helped the poor.

....

....

....

....

....

There are 12 marks on offer for this question. You don't have to use the prompts in the question but you **must** include your own information to answer the question fully.

....

....

....

....

....

Your explanations need to stay focused on answering the question. Although you might remember lots of detail about the dissolution of the monasteries, you have got to explain **how** the dissolution of the monasteries led to the Pilgrimage of Grace.

....

....

Practice

Use this page to continue your answer to question 4(b).

....
....
....
....
....
....
....
....
....
....
....
....
....
....
....
....
....
....
....
....
....
....
....
....
....
....
....
....
....

For example, you might explain that many people in the North of England had economic complaints. These included rising rents and higher taxes, especially the Statute of Uses (a tax on inheritance). This situation was made worse by poor harvests leading to rising food prices and food shortages.

Link your points together into a single argument using phrases such as 'This led to...' and 'This meant that...'.

Remember: the best answers to Question 4(b) will show a good knowledge of the key features and characteristics of the period **and** analyse causation. They will also show how factors combine with each other to bring about an outcome – so in this case how different factors come together to bring about the uprising.

Make sure you support your explanation with a good range of accurate and relevant detail throughout your answer.

Practice

Put your skills and knowledge into practice with the following question.

Answer EITHER 4(c)(i) OR 4(c)(ii).

EITHER

4 (c) (i) 'The main consequence of the break with Rome in 1534 was Henry's marriage to Anne Boleyn.'

How far do you agree? Explain your answer.

(16 marks)

You may use the following in your answer:

• Henry's divorce from Catherine of Aragon

• the Act of Supremacy (1534).

You **must** also use information of your own.

OR

4 (c) (ii) 'The main reason for the fall of Anne Boleyn in 1536 was her failure to produce a male heir.'

How far do you agree? Explain your answer.

(16 marks)

You may use the following in your answer:

• Anne's failure to produce a male heir

• the influence of the Seymours.

You **must** also use information of your own.

For **Question 4(c)**, you have a **choice of two questions**. Each question is worth the same number of marks. Although one might immediately seem a question you can answer, do read both carefully to check your choice is the right one.

On the exam paper, the two options for Question 4(c) will be on one page, and you will then turn to the next page to write your answer – like the layout here.

If you decide to answer question 4(c)(i), turn to page 42. If you decide to answer 4(c)(ii), turn to page 46.

Links You can revise the break with Rome on page 20. For more about the fall of Anne Boleyn, turn to page 14.

Choosing a question

At the top of the first answer page there will be an instruction for you to indicate which of the two questions you have chosen to answer. You do this by making a cross in the box for (c)(i) or (c)(ii). (You can see this on pages 42 and 46.)

Don't worry if you put a cross in the wrong box by mistake. Just put a line through the cross and then put a new cross in the correct box.

Practice

Put your skills and knowledge into practice with the following question.

Indicate which question you are answering by marking a cross in the box. If you change your mind, put a line through the box and then indicate your new question with a cross.

Remember **only** to answer **either** Question 4(c)(i) **or** Question 4(c)(ii) in the exam.

Chosen question: 4(c)(i) [x]   4(c)(ii) ☐

Plan your answer **before** you start writing. List factors that support the statement in the question, and list other factors that go against the statement.

Guided Henry's marriage to Anne Boleyn was a major consequence of the break with Rome. However, there were other consequences, including the Act of Supremacy (1534), Henry's control over Church finances and the dissolution of the monasteries.

For example:

Support	Against
Divorce from Catherine of Aragon	The Act of Supremacy, 1534
Act of Succession and marriage to Anne Boleyn	Control over Church finances – Court of First Fruits and Tenths; Court of Augmentations
	Dissolution of the monasteries

Spending a couple of minutes planning your answer means you can write an introduction setting up your arguments.

For each point you make, always then explain how it relates to the question.

Practice

Use this page to continue your answer to question 4(c)(i).

Guided Moreover, Henry's divorce from Catherine and
subsequent marriage to Anne Boleyn were not the only
consequences of the break with Rome. There was also the
Act of Supremacy (1534). This gave Henry, and not the
pope, complete control over the English Church.

As with question 4(b), you do not have to use both or either of the two prompts provided by the question. If you do use them, remember that you **must** also include information of your own.

End your answer by saying **how far** you agree with the question statement and give support for your decision.

Other consequences, such as the Act of Supremacy, were very important as they gave Henry control over Church finances.

In addition, Henry could use the power given to him by the Act of Supremacy to dissolve the monasteries, boosting his income and significantly affecting the lives of ordinary people who relied on them.

For example, you might conclude that, although the marriage to Anne Boleyn was an important consequence of the break with Rome, it was very short lived; Anne was executed in 1536.

Practice

Use this page to continue your answer to question 4(c)(i).

....

....

....

....

....

....

....

....

....

....

....

....

....

....

....

....

....

....

....

....

....

....

....

....

....

....

....

....

Practice

Use this page to continue your answer to question 4(c)(i).

Practice

Put your skills and knowledge into practice with the following question.

Indicate which question you are answering by marking a cross in the box. If you change your mind, put a line through the box and then indicate your new question with a cross.

Chosen question: 4(c)(i) ☐   4(c)(ii) ☒

Guided Anne's failure to produce an heir was a key reason
why she was executed in May 1536. However, other
reasons were also important. Henry's attraction to Jane
Seymour gave the Seymour family greater influence in court
and created a poisonous atmosphere that led to Anne's
downfall. Additionally, Cromwell is seen as deliberately
plotting against Anne, building a case of adultery against
her.

....
....
....
....
....
....
....
....
....
....
....
....
....
....
....
....
....

Remember: Question 4(c) gives you a choice of two questions. **In the exam, you only need to answer either 4(c)(i) or 4(c)(ii).**

This question asks about **reasons**: 'The main reason for the fall of Anne Boleyn in 1536 was her failure to produce a male heir.' Reasons are **why** something happened. You must give reasons for Anne's eventual execution in 1536.

For example, you might state that one reason for Anne's eventual downfall was her failure to produce a male heir. Henry was desperate for a male heir as the absence of one raised questions about his virility (manliness), while it also meant that the succession could be disputed after his death. Anne, by giving birth to a daughter, Elizabeth, as well as at least one further miscarriage, was disappointing to Henry, making him more willing to end his marriage.

You could mention the fact that Anne's failure to produce a male heir suggested to Henry that God disapproved of the marriage, proving that it had to end.

Practice

Use this page to continue your answer to question 4(c)(ii).

....

....

....

....

....

....

....

....

....

....

....

....

....

....

....

....

....

....

....

....

....

....

....

....

....

....

....

....

....

....

As with question 4(b), you do not have to use both or either of the two prompts provided by the question. If you do use them, remember that you **must** also include information of your own.

Bring specific facts and details into your answer to show how well you understand the key features and characteristics that are involved in the question.

When you end your answer, make sure you say **how far** you agree with the question statement and give support for your decision.

Practice

Use this page to continue your answer to question 4(c)(ii).

Practice

Use this page to continue your answer to question 4(c)(ii).

....
....
....
....
....
....
....
....
....
....
....
....
....
....
....
....
....
....
....
....
....
....
....
....
....
....
....
....
....
....

Answers

Where an exemplar answer has been provided, it does not necessarily represent the only correct response. In most cases there are a range of responses that can gain full marks.

SUBJECT CONTENT

Henry VIII and Wolsey, 1509–29

1. Society and government

Any two from the following:

- Only 6 per cent of the population lived in towns such as London, Norwich and Exeter. The rest lived in the countryside.
- Rural society was hierarchical. At the top, lay the nobility or major landowners, such as the Duke of Norfolk. Many held seats in the House of Lords and had places at court. Below the landowners, were the gentry who owned less land. Below the gentry, were the yeomen farmers who owned and farmed smaller amounts of land. Below the yeomen farmers, were the tenant farmers who rented the land they farmed often from the gentry and major landowners. Finally, there were the landless and labouring poor who were employed to work the land often by the yeomen and tenant farmers. At the very bottom, were the vagrants or homeless poor whose numbers grew across Henry VIII's reign.
- Urban society was also hierarchical. At the top, were merchants who traded goods with fellow merchants often from Spain, Russia and the Netherlands. Many were involved in the wool trade. Below the merchants, was the professional class including doctors and lawyers. Below the professionals, were small business owners, craftsmen (joiners, carpenters, etc. who served an apprenticeship), unskilled labourers and the unemployed.
- There was relatively little social mobility in Tudor society. This meant that most people did not leave the social class they were born into. People were expected to respect those above them and look after those below them.

2. Henry's accession

For example:

- Henry saw himself as a Renaissance man, modelling himself on the Renaissance monarchies of France and Spain. He saw himself as a man of learning, conversant in different foreign languages and interested in culture (art, music and dance).
- Henry also believed in the divine right of kings. This meant that he had been appointed by God to rule. This meant that he had an obligation to govern properly and people had an obligation to obey him.
- Henry used the Royal Council (later the Privy Council) to help him make decisions. He also liked to employ a chief minister. This was Wolsey and later Cromwell. Henry was also prepared to delegate

routine tasks that bored him to his ministers. This gave them considerable power and influence. Wolsey became known as *Alter Rex* or second king.

3. Henry's strengths, weaknesses and aims

Any two from the following:

- England was stable. There was now an established system of government and little threat of civil war.
- Henry's marriage to Catherine of Aragon gave him connections to Spain; a growing European power. This provided him with a potential ally against France and Scotland.
- Henry inherited a rich country. The Crown was not in debt, while the wool trade provided the king with extra revenue.
- Henry was a popular king. He was young and different from his father, Henry VII, who was disliked by many noblemen and merchants due to his taxes.
- Henry had experienced advisers around him, including Wolsey, who would help him govern the country.

4. Wolsey's rise to power

Any two from the following:

- Henry did not involve himself in day-to-day government, preferring instead to engage in jousting, hunting and other noble sports. This increased Wolsey's power as he was left to carry out the boring but important tasks which Henry wished to avoid doing himself.
- Wolsey's appointment as Royal Almoner in 1509 (in charge of donations to the poor) made him a member of the Royal Council, giving him regular access to the king. This gave him opportunities to impress and exert influence over Henry, enabling him to dominate government by 1515.
- Henry disliked many of his father's advisers who he saw as too cautious and unpopular. This removed potential rivals, easing Wolsey's path to power by 1515.
- Wolsey's persuasive personality and his use of flattery enabled him to exert influence over the king, while making him an effective negotiator on Henry's behalf. His ruthlessness and willingness to financially ruin his rivals deterred challengers, enabling him to accumulate power.
- Wolsey was ambitious, giving him the drive to accumulate power and influence under Henry.
- The war with France in 1512 enabled Wolsey to prove his worth to Henry by organising a well-equipped, well-supplied army by 1513. Wolsey demonstrated skills that Henry later relied on, increasing his power and influence at court.

5. Wolsey's reforms

Any two from the following:

- New taxes including the subsidy. This was a tax on incomes (what people earned). This was a progressive tax; the more you earned the more you paid.

- Wolsey, like his predecessors taxed the Church.
- Wolsey forced major landowners to lend the government money in 1522 and 1523.
- Wolsey ensured that the government obtained income from Crown lands. He also recovered Crown lands from the nobility. This meant that lands taken by the nobility were restored to the king. This raised £15 000 in 1515 alone.
- Wolsey reduced royal household expenditure through the Eltham Ordinances, which saved money on fuel, wages and food.

6. The Amicable Grant

Any one from the following short-term consequences:

- Many people refused to pay the tax, claiming that they had no money and could not afford to pay.
- A full-scale revolt broke out as people refused to pay a tax which they perceived to be unfair. For example, 10 000 gathering in Lavenham, Suffolk, expressed their loyalty to the king but demanded he be aware of their anger.
- Facing widespread anger over the tax, Henry was forced to issue a royal pardon to those who refused to pay it.
- Because the tax was uncollectable, Henry was forced to abandon it and, instead, made peace with France.

Any one from the following long-term consequences:

- Wolsey's reputation was badly damaged as he was deemed to be responsible for both the tax and the failure to collect it. He, rather than the king, had to take responsibility for the tax and its failure.
- The unpopularity of the tax meant that Wolsey was unable to raise any further taxes while he remained the king's first minister.
- Henry began, perhaps for the first time, to doubt Wolsey's judgement, beginning a process that would result in his fall from power.
- The position of Wolsey's enemies among the nobility in the royal court was strengthened. Wolsey's introduction of the Eltham Ordinances was perhaps an attempt to reduce their influence over the king.
- The failure of the Amicable Grant demonstrated that there were limitations to the king's power, as he could no longer raise taxes without the consent of parliament.

7. Wolsey's foreign policy aims

Wolsey was cautious about involving England in a long European war because wars were expensive. This meant that they had to be paid for normally by raising taxes. Excessive taxes, as the opposition to the Amicable Grant demonstrated, could undermine the popularity of the government and even lead to rebellion.

Wars were also risky. Defeat could lead to loss of territory and damage to the king's reputation in the eyes of his subjects, including the nobility.

8. Foreign policy outcomes

Wolsey's foreign policy ran into difficulties because of the unreliability of his allies leaving England diplomatically isolated in Europe.

Henry had assumed that he could play Europe's two main monarchs, Francis I and Charles V, off against each other. This was not the case. When England went to war with Charles V against Francis I in 1525, Henry assumed that he would get a share of the spoils of war (the division of France between Charles and Henry) following Charles' victory at the Battle of Pavia. Instead, Charles released Francis leaving Henry with a war that had cost £430 000 but had achieved little.

Similarly, in 1528, when Henry enlisted the help of France against the Habsburg alliance, Francis concluded the Treaty of Cambrai with Charles, leaving England diplomatically isolated.

9. Catherine of Aragon and the succession

The issue of the succession was important to Henry for a number of reasons. First, the failure to produce an heir reflected badly on the king's authority. It implied that he lacked the virility (manliness) required to produce an heir, undermining his kingship. Second, it suggested divine disfavour. Henry's failure to produce a male heir suggested that God was displeased with him, leading some to view him as a poor and sinful ruler, undermining his authority among his subjects and within the Church. Third, the succession was important to ensure the stability of the kingdom. The absence of a male heir would mean that, on Henry's death, the throne would be disputed leading to civil war. To resolve these issues and to preserve his authority, Henry required a male heir.

10. Attempts to gain an annulment

Any two from the following:

- Clement VII, following the Battle of Pavia, was in no position to grant an annulment as it would anger Charles V, Catherine's nephew. The pope was also reluctant to offend Henry, a key ally, so instead engaged in delaying tactics, frustrating Henry and Wolsey by refusing to come to a decision on the issue and in the end saying it was for Rome to decide after all.
- Catherine was resolutely opposed to the annulment and even publicly begged the king not to cast her aside. This made it harder for Henry to make a convincing case for annulment as he could not risk upsetting Charles V, Catherine's nephew, whose support he needed against the French king, Francis I.
- Catherine had supporters in the royal court including John Fisher, Bishop of Rochester, and Thomas More, adviser to the king. These were prepared to oppose the annulment both in the court and parliament.
- Catherine was popular with ordinary people. Henry recognised this and had to tread carefully in his dealings with Catherine, making it difficult to annul the marriage without papal approval.

11. Wolsey's fall from power

For example:
- The failure to secure an annulment of Henry's marriage to Catherine.
- The influence of the Boleyns.
- The failure of the Amicable Grant.
- A disastrous foreign policy.
- The failure of Wolsey's reforms.

Henry VIII and Cromwell, 1529–40

12. Cromwell's early career

Cromwell's ruthlessness was key to his rise to power. It meant that the king was prepared to rely on him to manage violent and controversial acts, for example the execution of court rivals, such as More, as well as the execution of Anne Boleyn and the dissolution of the monasteries. Cromwell's ruthlessness also discouraged rivals and opponents from challenging his rise to power.

However, there were other reasons for Cromwell's rise to power. By 1530, Henry was involving himself more in day-to-day government than was the case under Wolsey, where he was happy to let others act on his behalf. He seems to have seen Cromwell as someone who would carry out his instructions quickly and efficiently. Cromwell rose to power not as *Alter Rex* (Wolsey) but as the king's loyal servant.

Moreover, Cromwell remained loyal to Wolsey, defending him in parliament and even in audiences with the king. This loyalty seems to have impressed Henry, who was prepared to promote Cromwell on the grounds that he would be equally loyal to him; a servant of the king.

Finally, Cromwell's wit and charm was effective in succeeding where Wolsey had failed. His ability to persuade parliament to pass the Act in Restraint of Appeals paved the way for Henry's divorce from Catherine and marriage to Anne Boleyn, as well as the Acts of Succession and Supremacy. Henry was therefore willing to grant Cromwell more power as he exercised it effectively.

13. Cromwell and the king's annulment

The success of the annulment was beneficial to Cromwell as Henry entrusted him with further powers. He placed him in charge of the Church as the Vicar-General; he became in charge of the law as Master of the Rolls; he became in charge of the royal household as Lord Great Chamberlain; he became in charge of Henry's private documents as Lord Privy Seal; and as Chancellor of the Exchequer in charge of finances.

14. The fall of Anne Boleyn

Any two from the following:
- Henry's infatuation with Jane Seymour and his keenness to marry her made it necessary to get rid of Anne.
- Henry was exasperated by Anne's failure to give birth to a boy and made it necessary to replace her with another queen.
- Henry did not like the way Anne had strong opinions on foreign policy and religion – it wasn't thought seemly for a woman, let alone a queen, to have strong views.
- Anne was not popular in court and there were many allegations of adultery that Henry was happy to believe.

15. Jane Seymour

The birth of Edward VI was important because it provided Henry with a male heir. This reduced the possibility of a disputed succession and a civil war after Henry eventually died. It also suggested that God was pleased with Henry's conduct by rewarding him with an heir. This also seemed to suggest that all of the changes Henry had introduced, including the Act of Supremacy and the dissolution of the monasteries, were approved by God.

16. Cromwell's reforms

Any two from the following:
- Cromwell reformed the Royal Council. The unwieldy Royal Council, which contained up to 100 members, was replaced by a smaller permanent Privy Council of around 20. Moreover, the composition of the Privy Council was more professional, containing lawyers and professional administrators rather than noblemen and friends of the king.
- Cromwell reformed the Council of the North, turning it into a permanent institution responsible for maintaining law and order in the North of England.
- Cromwell also reformed the government of Wales. English law replaced Welsh law, while Wales was divided up into counties like England, each of which was controlled by a Justice of the Peace (JP). Wales was also divided up into constituencies, each of which sent MPs to parliament.
- Cromwell also reformed government finances and the King's Chamber. Traditionally, the King's Chamber was used to record the income (taxes, rents, etc) and expenditure (money spent) of the king and his government. Cromwell changed this by dividing the Chamber up into a number of different bodies and adding the Court of Augmentations (dealing with property and income from the dissolution of the monasteries) and the Court of First Fruits and Tenths (which collected taxes from the clergy previously sent to the pope). Each department had the power to settle financial disputes and was given its own budget. They were run by officials who were well trained and monitored.

17. The management and use of parliament

Any two from the following:
- It strengthened Henry's authority by establishing the idea of the king in parliament. This meant that any law proposed by the king or his ministers and passed by the House of Commons and the House of Lords could not be challenged.
- It meant that the sovereignty of the king – his authority to govern – was now wielded by parliament on the king's behalf. This meant that parliament could pass any law it liked as it had absolute legislative power.
- It also enhanced the importance of parliament. It could not be ignored by the king and his ministers and should be consulted on all major laws that the king wished to pass.

18. Anne of Cleves

The failure of the marriage between Anne and Henry was a disaster for Cromwell. Henry lost confidence in Cromwell as it was he who had organised the image of Anne that had persuaded Henry he would receive her, only to be disappointed when he actually saw her.

Once Cromwell had lost Henry's confidence and was seen not to be so popular in court, other courtiers saw their opportunity to pounce, in particular the Duke of Norfolk, the uncle of Catherine Howard, Henry's next interest. The failure also weakened Henry's interest in Protestantism and Cromwell was the main driver of this.

19. Cromwell's fall

- The Duke of Norfolk's ambitions and hatred of Cromwell. He stirred things up in court by spreading rumours against Cromwell.
- Cromwell was hated by the French. Getting rid of Cromwell would improve relations with France and reduce the threat of a Catholic crusade against England.
- Cromwell had enemies within the Church after the dissolution of the monasteries and the execution of Thomas More and John Fisher.

The Reformation and its impact, 1529–40

20. Henry and the Catholic Church

The pope's failure to annul Henry's marriage to Catherine of Aragon was an important reason for the break with Rome. It meant that he had to deny the pope's authority to get a divorce leading to the Act in Restraint of Appeals, the Act of Succession and the Act of Supremacy.

However, there were other reasons why Henry campaigned against the Catholic Church. Henry rejected many Protestant ideas, but liked the idea expressed by William Tyndale that God had always intended the Church to be ruled by kings. This pushed him towards wishing to take control of the Church himself. By having complete control of the Church in England, Henry would benefit from its wealth.

Allegations of corruption in the English Church gave Henry the excuse he needed to take control of the Church as a means of reforming it and getting his hands on its money.

21. The Acts of Succession and Supremacy

The Acts of Succession and Supremacy were important because they established the succession and gave Henry control over the Church. The Act of Succession stated that only children from Henry's marriage to Anne Boleyn could inherit the throne. This was important because it meant that Mary was now barred from the throne, while it was the king and parliament who could determine who Henry's successor was.

The Act of Supremacy was important because it meant that Henry VIII and not the pope now had control of the Church in England. This gave Henry control over the Church, including its beliefs, religious services and wealth.

22. Elizabeth Barton and John Fisher

The punishments were harsh because Henry wanted to:
- show people what could happen if they opposed his religious reforms
- avoid the possibility of rebellion from those who were unhappy with the reforms
- make sure people took the Oath of Succession.

23 Opposition from Thomas More

More was prepared to become a martyr for the Catholic cause. This meant that he was seen as someone who was prepared to give up his life for his beliefs and challenge Henry's authority over the Church. This potentially encouraged opposition from prominent Catholics at court, such as the Duke of Norfolk, as well as rebellion in the countryside.

More's stand potentially deepened the split with Rome, making a reconciliation between Henry and the pope more difficult.

24. The impact of the Reformation on the Church

There is considerable evidence that suggests that, by 1540, England was already becoming a Protestant country. Many Protestant ideas had established themselves within the Church. Only three sacraments existed: baptism; the Eucharist; and penance – implying that the Catholic idea of seven sacraments had been rejected. Protestant thinking was also reflected in the way that pilgrimages, relics and religious images were discouraged and were stated in Royal Injunctions. Moreover, the Bishops Book held that the main job of the clergy was preaching and a Royal Injunction in 1538 stated that a copy of the Bible was to be placed in all churches. Both these ideas were Protestant ideas associated with Martin Luther and William Tyndale who were prominent Protestants. Protestantism was also reflected in the Act of Supremacy and the Act in Restraint of Appeals, which both amounted to a rejection of the authority of the pope. Indeed, all clergy were required to declare allegiance to Henry as Head of the Church. Clergy who did not, such as John Fisher, were executed.

However, many Catholic ideas remained. The Six Articles published by Henry in 1539 reaffirmed traditional Catholic beliefs, such as transubstantiation, clerical celibacy and purgatory. Failure to agree to these would lead to imprisonment, confiscation of property and death. Indeed, clergy who preached against these ideas, such as John Lambert, were executed.

Overall, England was neither Catholic nor Protestant in 1540. The authority of the pope had been removed by the Act of the Supremacy, while Bibles were available in English churches. However, many Catholic ideas remained while Cromwell's death in 1540 weakened the Protestant cause in England.

25. The role of religious houses

For example:
- Monasteries had a medical role. They acted as hospitals and hospices looking after the sick and the dying.
- They acted as places of refuge. Monasteries were safe places where people could stay when they travelled. They also acted as safe havens for people who felt threatened.
- Monasteries had a social and economic role. Monasteries provided help for the poor. They also provided employment for local people who helped run the monasteries and maintain their lands.
- Many large monasteries acted as businesses controlling estates and renting out land to local farmers.

26. The dissolution of the monasteries

Financial reasons were important in Henry's decision to close down the monasteries. The monasteries were very wealthy. Henry's survey of the Church had established that the total income of the monasteries was £160 000 per year. Closing down the monasteries and taking over and renting out the monastic lands would pay for any future wars and for the defence of England against any Catholic crusade. It would also make Henry financially independent of parliament as he would no longer have to ask it to approve taxation. Land could also be sold off or given as gifts to the nobility.

However, there were also political and religious reasons for the dissolution. Many reformers, including Cromwell and Cranmer, disapproved of many of the religious practices in the monasteries. Getting rid of the monasteries would, in their view, end these backward practices.

Politically, Henry may have felt that many monks and nuns were loyal to the pope rather than the king. Closing down the monasteries would strengthen Henry's control of the Church by getting rid of sources of opposition within it.

Overall, financial reasons were important to the dissolution of the monasteries, but there were powerful political and religious reasons also.

27. Beneficiaries and losers

Those who benefited:
- Religious reformers.
- Henry VIII.
- The nobility.

Views on who benefited most and who benefited least will vary. To reach a decision, you should consider the following points:
- The king benefited enormously from the closure of the monasteries. He benefited from the fact that the monasteries' income of £160 000 a year was now paid to the government. This made him financially independent as he would no longer have to ask parliament for money through taxation.
- The closure of the monasteries also helped end opposition from within the Church to Henry's rule, strengthening the Act of Supremacy.
- Religious reformers like Cromwell and Cranmer benefited as the closure of the monasteries meant that a powerful symbol of the Catholic Church was brought to an end. This meant that dissolution was another step along the road towards a reformed Protestant Church.
- The nobility also benefited as they now received monastic lands from the king either as a gift or sold to them cheaply. They could now farm the land commercially, increasing their incomes and wealth.

28. Pilgrimage of Grace: reasons

The Pilgrimage of Grace was supported by all sections of society, from poor labourers to the gentry. This showed how important the monasteries were for everyone in the community, providing: education; care for the sick; places of refuge; employment; and religious instruction. With the dissolution of the monasteries many things that were important in a community were taken away, which led many people from all sectors of society determined to fight back.

29. Pilgrimage of Grace: key events

When the Duke of Norfolk met with the Pilgrimage of Grace at Doncaster Bridge on 27 October 1536, he realised he was outnumbered and was unlikely to defeat the well-organised Pilgrim armies. Defeat would have been very embarrassing for Henry and the Duke, and would have seriously affected the king's authority and power. A way out of the situation was to offer to enter into negotiations, which duly occurred.

30. Failure of the uprising

Robert Aske's willingness to put his faith in the king was a key reason why the Pilgrimage of Grace failed. He disbanded his army before securing the agreement with Henry, when he should have maintained the threat to force Henry's hand. However, Henry's ruthlessness did not help Aske. Henry wanted to demonstrate that he was a strong monarch who could face down rebellion. He could not concede the rebel's demands as this would have made him appear weak, encouraging others to challenge his authority. It would also have completely undermined his religious policy.

PRACTICE

38. Practice

4(a) For each feature, you get one mark for identifying the feature up to a maximum of two features, and one mark for adding supporting information.

For example:
- The Treaty of London (1518) required each of the 20 countries who signed it to pursue a non-aggressive foreign policy. This meant that they could no longer use force to achieve their goals.
- The Treaty of London established a system of collective security. If one power went to war, it risked being attacked by the other countries who had signed the treaty. This deterred countries from using warfare to achieve their goals.

39. Practice

4(b) There are 6 marks on offer for AO1 and 6 marks for AO2 in this question. If you do not introduce your own information then you can only get a maximum of 8 marks. Your AO1 information needs to be accurate and relevant and for AO2 you need to provide an explanation.

For example:
There were a number of different reasons for the Pilgrimage of Grace in 1536. These were religious, financial, social and political.

In the North of England, including Lincolnshire, Yorkshire and Durham, many opposed Henry's religious changes, including the dissolution of the monasteries as well as the end of Holy Days and pilgrimages. Many felt that attacks on Parish churches would follow. The Pilgrimage was an attempt to reverse these changes and protect the 'old religion' from further attack.

Linked to these were social reasons. The monasteries benefited many local communities as they provided employment, care for the sick, a place of refuge and help for the poor. Their dissolution provoked widespread anger in Lincolnshire and Yorkshire leading to rebellion by 1536.

This anger was made worse by financial change. Bad harvests, continuing taxation and rising rents were all sources of discontent in the North, while many landowners opposed the Statute of Uses; a tax on inheritances. The Pilgrimage reflected widespread dissatisfaction with these economic circumstances.

This willingness to confront the king was strengthened by political dissatisfaction. Many members of the northern nobility resented the influence of Cromwell, as well as his low birth and reformist (Protestant) ideas. The rebellion was an attempt to weaken Cromwell's influence at court and strengthen that of the northern nobility.

41. Practice

4(c)(i) This question has 16 marks on offer: 6 for AO1 and 10 for AO2. Your task is to evaluate the statement and come to a conclusion about how far you agree with it, justifying the conclusion you reach. This means considering how important the consequence or reason given in the statement is compared to other consequences or reasons.

For example:
Henry's marriage to Anne Boleyn was a major consequence of the break with Rome. However, there were other consequences including the Act of Supremacy (1534), Henry's control over Church finances and the dissolution of the monasteries.

The marriage to Anne Boleyn did result from the break with Rome. Before Henry passed the Act in Restraint of Appeals, only the pope could annul Henry's marriage to Catherine of Aragon. However, the Act meant that it was the king and not the pope who could decide this matter. This resulted in Henry's secret marriage to Anne (she was already pregnant) and the Act of Succession, which made the children of Anne and not Catherine the heirs to the English throne. However, this was only a short-term consequence of the break with Rome. Anne was executed in 1536 and replaced by Jane Seymour.

Moreover, Henry's divorce from Catherine and subsequent marriage to Anne Boleyn were not the only consequences of the break with Rome. There was also the Act of Supremacy (1534). This gave Henry, and not the pope, complete control over the English Church. This meant that it was the king and not the pope who controlled the Church's property, beliefs and practices.

This had far-reaching consequences as it meant that Church revenues went to Henry rather than the pope, resulting in the setting up of the Court of Augmentations and the Court of First Fruits and Tenths, which controlled the money coming in to Henry's government from the Church. It also led to a change in religious services with seven sacraments (the Roman Catholic tradition) being replaced by three (the Eucharist, baptism and penance), as well as an emphasis on preaching and a Bible being placed in each English church.

Most importantly of all, it enabled Henry to dissolve the monasteries between 1535 and 1539. Monastic lands were now placed at the disposal of the king, increasing his wealth dramatically. It also meant that he was no longer so reliant on parliament for taxation and could build up his support among the nobility by giving or selling them land.

In conclusion, Henry's marriage to Anne was only a short-term consequence of the break with Rome. Of more importance were its long-term consequences, including the Act of Supremacy and the dissolution of the monasteries.

46. Practice

4(c)(ii) This question has 16 marks on offer: 6 for AO1 and 10 for AO2. Your task is to evaluate the statement and come to a conclusion about how far you agree with it, justifying the conclusion you reach. This means considering how important the consequence or reason given in the statement is compared to other consequences or reasons.

For example:
Anne's failure to produce an heir was a key reason why she was executed in May 1536. However, other reasons were also important. Henry's attraction to Jane Seymour gave the Seymour family greater influence in court and created a poisonous atmosphere that led to Anne's downfall. Additionally, Cromwell is seen as deliberately plotting against Anne, building a case of adultery against her.

For Henry, a male heir was key to the future of the Tudor dynasty. A male heir would guarantee the succession and make a civil war on Henry's death less likely. It would also boost Henry's authority by demonstrating his virility as well as divine approval of the marriage. Anne's failure to produce a male heir was therefore frustrating to Henry. The fact that Anne's only child, Elizabeth, was female, coupled with at least two further miscarriages, may have convinced Henry that the marriage was barren, creating a need to be rid of Anne. This frustration may have been enhanced by Anne's flirtatious behaviour, which resulted in rumours at court, creating the impression in his mind that she could not be trusted and that God's disapproval of both Anne and the marriage was denying him a male heir.

However, there were other reasons for Anne's fall from power. Henry's increasing attraction to Jane Seymour increased the influence of the Seymour family at court. They were more than happy to bring about Anne's downfall as a means of ensuring that Jane became Henry's wife. To this end, they contributed to the poisonous atmosphere at court that led to rumour and innuendo directed at Anne, leading to her eventual execution.

Linked to this was the role of Cromwell. He had already noted how the Boleyns had contributed to the downfall of Wolsey in 1529 and did not want to suffer the same fate. To this end, he was prepared to conspire against Anne, building a case that she had already slept with a number of courtiers including her own brother. Cromwell, it appears, was involved in this process which involved the torture and confession of a musician, Mark Smeaton, and resulted in Anne's trial and execution in May 1536.

Notes

Notes

Notes

Notes

Notes

Notes

Published by Pearson Education Limited, 80 Strand, London, WC2R 0RL.

www.pearsonschoolsandfecolleges.co.uk

Copies of official specifications for all Pearson qualifications may be found on the website: qualifications.pearson.com

Text and illustrations © Pearson Education Ltd 2017
Typeset and illustrated by Tech-Set, Ltd.
Produced by Tech-Set, Ltd.
Cover illustration by Eoin Coveney

The right of Brian Dowse to be identified as author of this work has been asserted by him in accordance with the Copyright, Designs and Patents Act 1988.

Content written by Rob Bircher, Victoria Payne and Kirsty Taylor is included.

First published 2017

20 19 18
10 9 8 7 6 5 4 3

British Library Cataloguing in Publication Data
A catalogue record for this book is available from the British Library

ISBN 9781292176390

Copyright notice
All rights reserved. No part of this publication may be reproduced in any form or by any means (including photocopying or storing it in any medium by electronic means and whether or not transiently or incidentally to some other use of this publication) without the written permission of the copyright owner, except in accordance with the provisions of the Copyright, Designs and Patents Act 1988 or under the terms of a licence issued by the Copyright Licensing Agency, Barnard's Inn, 86 Fetter Lane, London EC4A 1EN (www.cla.co.uk). Applications for the copyright owner's written permission should be addressed to the publisher.

Printed in Slovakia by Neografia

Acknowledgements
The publisher would like to thank the following for their kind permission to reproduce their photographs:

(Key: b-bottom; c-centre; l-left; r-right; t-top)

123RF.com: Alexey Fedorenko 4t; **Alamy Stock Photo:** Artokoloro Quint Lox Limited 21, Chronicle 3tr, G L Archive 2, 12, 15, Granger Historical Archive 3bl, Heritage Image Partnership Ltd 19, PRISMA ARCHIVO 17, V&A Images 18; **Bridgeman Art Library Ltd:** Birmingham Museums and Art Gallery 10, Hever Castle, Kent, UK 11bl, 13, His Grace The Duke of Norfolk, Arundel Castle 28t, Magdalen College, Oxford 4b, 11tl, Musee de Blois, Blois, France 23b, Nostell Priory, Yorkshire, UK / National Trust Photographic Library / John Hammond 23t, Private Collection / © Look and Learn 28b, Private Collection / Photo © Philip Mould Ltd, London 9, 11cr, Richard Bond / Private Collection / © Historic England 25, The French Hospital, Rochester, Kent, UK 27, Universal History Archive 14; **Fotolia.com:** orxy 26

All other images © Pearson Education

Notes from the publisher
1.
In order to ensure that this resource offers high-quality support for the associated Pearson qualification, it has been through a review process by the awarding body. This process confirms that this resource fully covers the teaching and learning content of the specification or part of a specification at which it is aimed. It also confirms that it demonstrates an appropriate balance between the development of subject skills, knowledge and understanding, in addition to preparation for assessment.

Endorsement does not cover any guidance on assessment activities or processes (e.g. practice questions or advice on how to answer assessment questions), included in the resource nor does it prescribe any particular approach to the teaching or delivery of a related course.

While the publishers have made every attempt to ensure that advice on the qualification and its assessment is accurate, the official specification and associated assessment guidance materials are the only authoritative source of information and should always be referred to for definitive guidance.

Pearson examiners have not contributed to any sections in this resource relevant to examination papers for which they have responsibility.

Examiners will not use endorsed resources as a source of material for any assessment set by Pearson.

Endorsement of a resource does not mean that the resource is required to achieve this Pearson qualification, nor does it mean that it is the only suitable material available to support the qualification, and any resource lists produced by the awarding body shall include this and other appropriate resources.

2.
Pearson has robust editorial processes, including answer and fact checks, to ensure the accuracy of the content in this publication, and every effort is made to ensure this publication is free of errors. We are, however, only human, and occasionally errors do occur. Pearson is not liable for any misunderstandings that arise as a result of errors in this publication, but it is our priority to ensure that the content is accurate. If you spot an error, please do contact us at resourcescorrections@pearson.com so we can make sure it is corrected.